# INTERNET TOOLS

**10 HOUR SERIES**

Herbert F. Brown, Ph.D.
Assistant Professor
Administrative Information Management
University of South Carolina
Columbia, South Carolina

SOUTH-WESTERN

THOMSON LEARNING

Australia • Canada • Mexico • Singapore • Spain • United Kingdom • United States

**SOUTH-WESTERN**
™
**THOMSON LEARNING**

*Internet Tools, 10-Hour Series*
By Dr. Herbert F. Brown

**Vice President/Executive Publisher:**
Dave Shaut

**Team Leader:**
Karen Schmohe

**Project Manager:**
Jane Congdon

**Consulting Editor:**
Elaine Langlois

**Editor:**
Carol Spencer

**Executive Marketing Manager:**
Carol Volz

**Channel Manager:**
Nancy Long

**Marketing Coordinator:**
Cira Brown

**Production Manager:**
Tricia Boies

**Manufacturing Manager:**
Charlene Taylor

**Design Project Manager:**
Stacy Jenkins Shirley

**Cover and Internal Design:**
Joseph Pagliaro

**Compositor:**
settingPace

**Printer:**
Courier Kendallville, Inc.

**Rights and Permissions Manager:**
Linda Ellis

For more information, contact:
South-Western Educational and
Professional Publishing
5101 Madison Road
Cincinnati, OH 45227-1490.
Or, visit our Internet site at
http://www.swep.com.

For permission to use material from
this text or product, contact us by
Phone: 1-800-730-2214,
Fax: 1-800-730-2215, or
http://www.thomsonrights.com.

# Preface

## Welcome to Internet Tools

The Internet is rapidly becoming an essential communications medium for the home and business environments. Being able to utilize Internet tools has become a necessity in many careers in today's technology-infused society. In every area of an organization, employees utilize the Internet for information retrieval and general communications. People are using Internet tools for research, shopping, travel planning, entertainment, education, investing, and communication.

In just ten hours, this book will teach you to use Internet tools to obtain information and Internet-based resources more efficiently. In just ten hours, you will be refining searches to find more information, listening to music online, planning upcoming travel adventures, and exploring online investment opportunities.

The ability to efficiently use the wide range of Internet tools available involves knowing what the tools are, where to find them, and how to use them. *Internet Tools* teaches these skills in an easy-to-follow format in ten lessons.

## Features

*Internet Tools* provides these useful features:

- A Focus quotation or activity to get you started on the lesson
- A lesson Overview and a Conclusion that summarizes what was covered
- An activity-driven approach with brief content and four to eight activities in each lesson
- Relevant and instructional illustrations
- Individual and team activities
- A Quick Reference Guide of web sites

## About the Author

Herb Brown is an Assistant Professor in the Administrative Information Management Program at the University of South Carolina. Dr. Brown has taught students and faculty at the college level for several years. He has also conducted numerous in-service training sessions for public school teachers and workshops on web page development and the Internet at the prestigious North Carolina Center for the Advancement of Teaching. Dr. Brown earned Bachelor of Science, Master of Science, and Doctor of Philosophy degrees in Business and Computer Education from Virginia Polytechnic Institute and State University. He has presented at numerous conferences and has published in his field. He is the author of *Web Page Design,* another 10-Hour Series text from South-Western Educational Publishing, and a contributing author to other South-Western texts.

Dr. Brown is married and has two boys. He currently resides in the Columbia area and looks forward to taking up the sport of kayaking after the completion of this book.

# Contents

# 1 Tools for the Job

## Focus

Getting information off the Internet is like taking a drink from a fire hydrant.

—Mitch Kapor

## Overview

No matter what job you are trying to accomplish, having the right tools makes the job easier. Using the Internet is no different. The **Internet** is the vast array of data links that connect millions of computer systems in a common format so that people can gain access to resources stored on those systems.

Most people today use the graphical portion of the Internet called the **World Wide Web.** This is not, however, the only part of the Internet. The Internet continues to host other systems such as e-mail, Internet Relay Chat (IRC), instant messaging, file transfer protocol (FTP), and Gopher. By one research company's estimate, as of mid-2000 there were 2.1 billion pages on the Internet, with some 7.3 million added each day.

Both the Internet and the World Wide Web are rapidly changing. Even as this book is being written, new technologies are being developed to utilize the power of this global computer network. The questions today are how will we use the Internet and how will we find what we need in its huge expanse of information resources?

In the next ten hours, you will learn what you need to know to use the Internet effectively in school, at work, and in your personal life. You will learn what kinds of resources are available on the Net, how to optimize searches, and where to look for information. You will learn to communicate using e-mail and applications like IRC and instant messaging tools.

You will also learn to locate and enjoy music with programs such as the RealPlayer® digital media software application and Microsoft® Windows Media™ Player. You will learn how to set up your own digital picture galleries on the Net and how to engage in safe, smart online shopping and investing. You will learn how to keep your computer system up to date and virus-free by downloading files and software. In the next ten hours, you will gather the tools and develop the skills you need to effectively use the Internet and its vast resources.

## Browsers

The first tool in your toolkit is the most important since most other tools rely on it, to some extent, to function properly. This tool is the browser. A **browser** provides you with a graphical interface for navigating the World Wide Web and other Internet resources.

The most commonly used browsers today are Netscape Navigator® and Microsoft® Internet Explorer. One new player in the browser market that is quickly making inroads is Opera by

Opera Software. This browser is becoming popular for several reasons, not the least being that it runs efficiently on almost any operating system, including the BeOS®, Linux, and Mac® OS operating systems.

Browsers are very similar in design and function. The **title bar** at the top of your browser window gives the names of the browser and the web page being viewed. The window includes a **menu bar** and a **toolbar.** There are **scroll bars** you can use to move through a page. Your window includes a text box that might be labeled *Address, Location, Go to,* or *Netsite* in different browsers. Here you key the **URL (Uniform Resource Locator)**, or address, for the web page you want to visit (for example, http://www.cnn.com). In many browsers, you don't have to key the **http://** or **www** part of the URL.

Figure 1 shows the toolbar from Opera. If you have a different browser, you may notice that the tools in your browser toolbar are similar. In fact, most browsers share a set of simple tools that help you navigate the Internet easily. Table 1 lists some common browser tools and describes what they do.

Figure 1 The Opera Browser Toolbar

| TOOL | FUNCTION |
|---|---|
| Home | Takes you back to your home page |
| Back | Takes you back one web page |
| Forward | Takes you forward one web page |
| Stop | Stops a page from loading (saves time) |
| Search | Takes you to a list of search tools (more on these below) |
| Print | Prints the page or set of pages |
| Reload or Refresh | Updates the page you are viewing |

Table 1 Common Browser Tools

Your browser will also have a **Bookmarks** or **Favorites** feature that lets you make a list of hyperlinks to web pages you visit often, so you do not have to key the URL each time you want to go to a page. Your Bookmarks or Favorites feature may have some popular web pages already installed. You can easily add pages to and delete pages from your Bookmarks or Favorites list. You can also organize pages into folders.

One helpful browser feature that many people don't know about is **History.** History is a toolbar button in some browsers and a menu option in others. This feature provides a list of hyperlinks

to pages you have visited in the recent past. Perhaps you visited a page and, a few days later, would like to return to it but can't remember what it was. You can find the page in History.

Another useful tool is the **Find** or **Find in Page** option in the Edit menu. This works like the word processing feature of the same name. You can use it to go directly to what interests you on a page instead of having to scan through a lot of material.

If you try different browsers, you may find that you prefer the features of one to another, but you can use any of these browsers to navigate the Internet easily. If you are running an older version of a browser, you may want to consider upgrading to a newer version. We'll discuss this in Lesson 10.

If you do not have a web browser, you can obtain one for minimal cost or in most cases, free. Many computers come with browser software already installed. You can go to a browser software manufacturer's web site and download a new browser or an upgraded version of your current browser. You can also purchase browser software at a **brick-and-mortar** (physical) store or online. Regardless of how you get your browser, you must have one, as it is your primary Internet tool.

## Search Tools

With so many pages throughout the entire Internet, how do you find what you are looking for? **Search tools**—programs that search the Internet for you—were developed just for that purpose. Hundreds of search tools are available on the Internet. Which one should you use? Aren't they all the same?

They are not all the same. Each search tool indexes the Internet in a different way. You can conduct a search with one tool and get no **hits,** or pages that match your search request, while another search tool produces dozens of hits to useful locations.

There are two basic types of search tools. **Categorical indexes** are collections of sites organized into categories and subcategories. Users find pages by

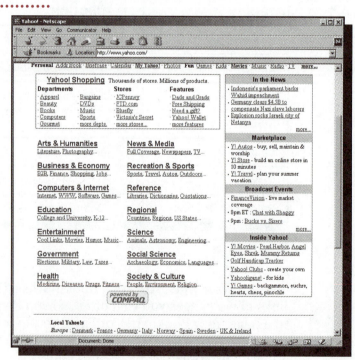

**Figure 2 A Categorical Index**

selecting categories and subcategories and browsing through the listings. Yahoo!® (Figure 2) and LookSmart are two popular categorical indexes.

Categorical indexes are helpful for finding general information on a subject. They are also good starting points for browsing. The pages included in a categorical index have been chosen by a team of editors, so they are often useful and trustworthy.

**Search engines** search an extensive database that contains all the text of millions of pages on the Internet for keywords you specify. They then return a list of pages that contain those keywords, with the most likely or closest matches listed first. Figure 3 shows a search engine with search results listed accordingly.

Search engines are useful when you are looking for specific information. They also provide access to more pages on the Internet than categorical indexes do. A growing number of search tools provide both categorical indexes and search engines for the user's convenience.

How can you search multiple search engines at one time? **Meta search engines** are the answer to this question. A meta search engine **queries** (or sends your search terms to) several different search engines at once. The meta search engine then displays the results of all the searches in one easy-to-read screen. Figure 4 displays a search result for the Dogpile meta search engine. Notice how the hits are categorized by search engine.

Meta search engines are the search tools of choice for many Internet users because you can search dozens of

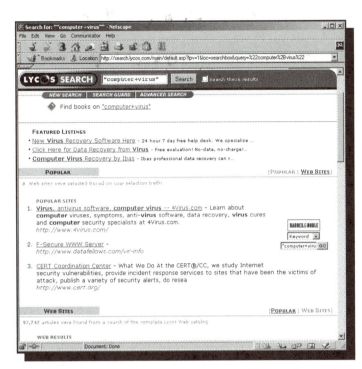

**Figure 3** Search Results in the LYCOS® Search Engine[1]

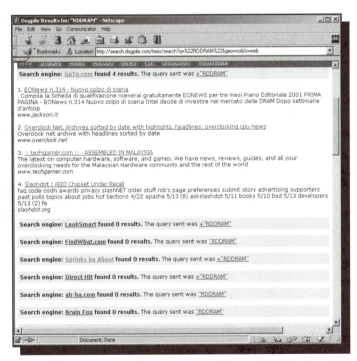

**Figure 4** Search Results in Dogpile

---

[1] LYCOS® is a registered trademark of Carnegie Mellon University in the United States and other countries.

search engines at one location in a fraction of the time it would take otherwise. In Figure 4, notice the number of search engines that Dogpile searched.

As you begin to search the Internet, try using different search tools. You will soon become familiar with the capabilities and features of different search engines and will find the ones that work best for you.

# Search Strategies

When you are using a search engine, how do you find the *specific* information you are looking for? Searches often return hundreds or thousands of hits, most of which are not what you want. The key to making the Internet a useful tool for you is to learn to efficiently and effectively form your search phrases so that the information returned is the most specific and useful.

When choosing your search terms, make sure you are as specific as possible. Try also to choose words that are unique—that are likely to be found in the pages you seek but not in other pages. The more specific and unique the words, the more likely you are to get the most appropriate hits. For example, if you are looking for information on computer memory and enter *computer memory* in a search engine, you will get hundreds of hits that are not what you are looking for. If you can use a more specific and unique term—*RDRAM,* for example—you will more quickly find useful information.

For many searches, simply choosing specific and unique keywords will yield the results you want. Table 2 lists some more ways to refine your search.

| SEARCH FOR | EXPLANATION |
|---|---|
| **Singular, plural** <br> *virus, viruses* | If a search for a singular noun (*virus*) doesn't yield enough results, try searching on the plural (*viruses*). If a search for a plural noun doesn't yield enough results, search on the singular. |
| **"Word word"** <br> *"computer virus"* | Finds pages that contain the words between quotation marks in order. For example, "*computer virus*" yields pages that contain the word *computer* followed by the word *virus,* not pages with the words in the other order or alone. |
| **Word +(plus) word** <br> *virus +computer* | Finds pages that contain both words |
| **Word –(minus) word** <br> *virus –computer* | Finds pages that contain the first word but not the second. For example, *virus –computer* returns hits on viruses but not on computer viruses. |

Table 2 **Tips for Refining Searches**

If these tips don't produce the results you desire, consider using the advanced search feature provided by many search engines. On the search engine home page, look for a link to *advanced search* options. These options might allow you to specify categories of links to search, such as images, newsgroups, or sounds. They might let you sort results by date or use other methods like those in Table 2 to narrow your search. One or more of these options are sometimes available directly on the home page of the search engine.

Also look for *help* links. These links will provide you with specific ways to optimize your search for that particular search engine. Here are a few more suggestions for smart searching.

- To find the web site for a company, product, college or university, or government agency, you can often key the name directly, using the format in Table 3.

- In most search engines, you do not need to capitalize words. You get the same results for *hawaii* as you would for *Hawaii*.

- Many search engines ignore common words like *the, and, how,* and *where.*

| URL FORMAT | | EXAMPLE |
|---|---|---|
| http://www.companyname.com | → | www.gap.com |
| http://www.productname.com | → | www.wheaties.com |
| http://www.schoolname.edu | → | www.mit.edu |
| http://www.governmentagency.gov | → | www.epa.gov |

Table 3  Key for Web Sites

# Conclusion

We began our discussion with the primary Internet tool—the browser. We have also discussed different types of search tools and strategies for finding Internet-based resources through search engines and meta search engines. Understanding how to use these tools lays the foundation for your exploration in the following lessons of many other tools the Internet has in store for you.

## Activity 1-1: Know Your Browser

Some browser programs include a built-in tour. Take a tour of your browser, if available. Use the tour and/or Help to explore some useful features of your browser software. At the keyboard, compose brief summaries (one to three sentences each) for two features you think will be helpful to you.

## Activity 1-2: Browser Power

In this activity, you will practice using the features of your browser to navigate the Internet.

1.  You are going to Chicago, and you want to visit the Museum of Science and Industry. Go to the museum web site at http://www.msichicago.org.

2.  The museum home page contains hyperlinks to a number of pages about the museum. Use these links and your browser navigation features to answer the following questions:

    a.  What are the museum's hours on weekdays? _____

    b.  You are planning to visit on a Thursday. What is the admission price? _____

    c.  Write down directions for getting to the museum by Metra (commuter rail).

    _____

    _____

    d.  Explore several of the online exhibits. List two that you would like to visit.

    _____

3.  You also want to go to the Sears Tower. Use a search engine to find the Sears Tower web site. Go to the site and answer the following questions:

    a.  How tall is the Sears Tower (including the twin antenna towers)? _____

    b.  How far can you see from the Skydeck on a clear day? _____

    c.  What states can you see from the Skydeck on a clear day?

    _____

4.  Print directions for getting to the Sears Tower from the Loop and parking nearby.

    _____

**Tools for the Job**

# Activity 1-3: Use the Bookmarks or Favorites and History Features

1. Learn how to use the Bookmarks or Favorites feature of your browser.

2. Visit the following sites. Add two of the sites to your list of Bookmarks or Favorites.

   http://www.espn.com                http://www.petersons.com
   http://www.historyplace.com        http://www.cnn.com
   http://moneycentral.msn.com        http://www.nationalgeographic.com

3. Find two additional sites that you like. Add them to your list of Bookmarks or Favorites.

4. Use the Bookmarks or Favorites feature to access two of the sites that you added.

5. Learn how to use the History feature of your software.

6. Open the History feature and examine the list of sites you have visited. Use the History feature to go to one of these sites.

# Activity 1-4: Search Smart

In this activity, you will practice some of the search strategies you learned in this lesson.

1. You are redoing your resume, and you want some tips. Go to the categorical index Yahoo!® at http://www.yahoo.com.

2. Under **Business & Economy,** click the **Employment and Work** and **Careers and Jobs** links.

3. Find and print information on preparing a resume.

4. You want to find a good web page for basketball statistics. Go to the categorical index LookSmart at http://www.looksmart.com.

5. Under **Sports,** click on **Basketball** and then on **Basketball Stats.** Write down a good URL.

   _____

6. Go to the meta search engine Dogpile at http://www.dogpile.com.

   a. You have to write a report on a Russian leader. Search for *Russian leader*. Notice your search results.

b. Now search for *Russian leaders*. Notice how the search results changed. Write down a promising URL.

_____

c. You want some information on how damaging computer viruses can be. Search for *computer virus*.

d. Now search for *computer virus +melissa*. This search yields very specific information about the Melissa computer virus. Write down the URL of a helpful site.

_____

7. You're thinking of buying a Ford truck. Go to the search engine Google (http://www.google.com).

a. Search for *Ford vehicles*. Notice the search results.

b. Now search for *Ford trucks*. Notice how you get more specific results.

c. Now search for *Ford F-150 4WD truck reviews*. Notice how specific your search results have become. Print one review.

8. Search for places where you can buy the movie *The Wizard of Oz* with Judy Garland and Ray Bolger. Write down a URL and the price of the movie.

_____

9. Search for sites where you can buy a kit to build a wooden touring kayak. Print the details for one model. Compare your results with those of your fellow students.

## Activity 1-5: Search-Engine Savvy

1. Go to the search engine AltaVista at http://www.altavista.com. Use the advanced search feature to locate music sites with MP3 clips of your favorite music artist. Print the first page of listings.

2. Go to the search engine Excite at http://www.excite.com. Select the **News** option. Search for news stories about a current event of your choosing. Print one story.

# Activity 1-6: Scavenger Hunt

In this activity, you will apply your search skills in an Internet scavenger hunt.

1. Find the date and time of the next scheduled space shuttle launch.

   _____

2. Get tomorrow's weather forecast for Columbia, South Carolina.

   _____

3. Use the following ticker symbols to find the current price per share for each stock.

   DAL _____        KO _____

   SNE _____        LTD _____

4. Find a site that gives product reviews for cellular phones. Write down the URL.

   _____

5. Go to the *Los Angeles Times* web site and print one of today's top stories.

6. Find a web site that lists apartments for rent in your town or in a town where you would like to live. Print a listing that interests you.

7. What were the years of birth and death for the poet William Butler Yeats?

   _____

8. Find the web site for the computer company that makes the computer you are working on. Record the URL.

   _____

9. Locate an online radio station that plays music you like to listen to. Record the URL.

   _____

10. Find and print a recipe for haggis and a recipe for carrot cake.

# 2 Research on the Net

## Focus

Knowledge is of two kinds. We know a subject ourselves, or we know where we can find information upon it.

—Samuel Johnson

According to a 2000 Gallup poll, 95 percent of Americans who use the Internet use it to obtain information.

## Overview

Now that you have the first tools to get started, the next question is, what can you use the Internet for? The Internet is rapidly becoming the location of choice for conducting research for school, work, or personal use. At your fingertips are dictionaries, encyclopedias, magazines, scholarly journals, newspapers, books, libraries, tutors, museums, laboratories, and an almost limitless number of other resources from around the world, many of which would not be available to you in any other way.

In seconds, you can find which animal species are endangered in Florida, what a restrictive clause is, and how much a dollar's worth of goods bought in 1954 would cost today. You can dissect a virtual frog, interview a famous scientist, and compare the performance of stocks. You can get help with your algebra homework, peruse job openings in Spokane, Washington, and research your family roots. You can find recent articles on acid rain, plan a trip to Australia, get weather information for that trip, and get biographical information on Marion Wright Edelman. This lesson will give you an overview of the resources available to you on the Internet for school, work, and personal research.

## Libraries

Libraries have always been the place to go to conduct research. The Internet gives us access to thousands of library computer systems around the world, including the Library of Congress system at http://www.loc.gov (Figure 1). Some resources are available online. For others, you may have to physically visit the library, have the resource delivered to your local library through a loan process, or have it copied for a nominal fee. There are also libraries that exist only on the Internet, where all materials are available online, such as the Internet Public Library (http://www.ipl.org).

With the Internet, you won't often have to go to a library to do research. Almost anything you used to visit the local library for can be accessed online.

**Reference Desks.** At a local library, people go to the reference desk to get answers to all sorts of questions and access to many different kinds of reference materials. The World Wide Web offers virtual reference desks, one-stop sites that serve as resources for many research needs. One example is http://www.refdesk.com.

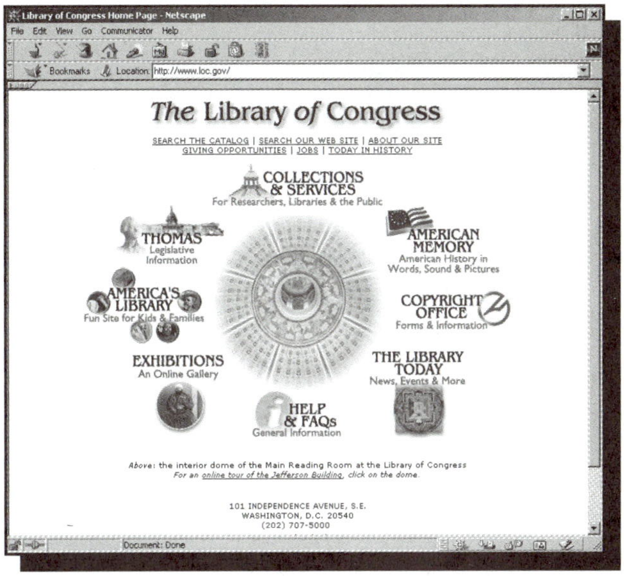

**Encyclopedias.** For many kinds of research, encyclopedias are an excellent place to begin. Many online encyclopedias offer resources that print encyclopedias cannot, such as sound clips, video, and vivid graphics. Several very good encyclopedias are available online. Two of these are *Encyclopedia Britannica* at http://www.britannica.com and the Microsoft® *Encarta*® online encyclopedia at http://encarta.msn.com.

**Dictionaries.** When you need to look up a word, you run for the dictionary. Now you can run to the Internet instead and search the *Merriam-Webster Collegiate*® *Dictionary* online at http://www.m-w.com. Yahoo!® offers an excellent collection of dictionaries on many subjects at its web site (http://www.yahoo.com; under **Reference,** choose **Dictionaries**).

**Figure 1** The Library of Congress Web Site

**Online Databases.** Hundreds of online databases exist on the Internet. Some are public. Many are private, and you must subscribe to them in order to gain access to their resources. Public databases are still filled with tomes of information. Many government and other organizational databases are online. To find databases, you can use the search tools you learned about in Lesson 1. However, a more direct approach may be to access library web pages and look for a link to electronic databases.

# Newspapers, Magazines, and Other Media

All major newspapers have web sites where you can browse current news articles or search for stories on specific topics. Two examples are *The New York Times* at http://www.nytimes.com and the *Los Angeles Times* at http://www.latimes.com. Many local newspapers are also available online. You can access newspapers from around the country and around the world at the *American Journalism Review*™ web site at http://www.ajr.org or at http://www.newspapers.com. Many newspapers let you search their archives and read summaries of older articles for free, but you usually have to pay a nominal price to retrieve the full text of an article. Newer articles (less than two weeks old) are generally available free online.

Many magazines can also be explored online. The best way to find a magazine is to search for it by name in a search tool. Some sites, such as http://www.newspapers.com, list magazine web

sites. Magazine web sites offer some of the content of print issues, such as excerpts from articles, and other materials as well, like audio and video clips.

Some scholarly journals are also available on the web. To find online journals, use search tools to locate them by name. You may also be able to use a journal index on a library web site to locate scholarly journals.

A great number of television and radio stations have an online component. Some examples are the Public Broadcasting System's web site at http://www.pbs.org and the British Broadcasting Corporation's web site at http://news.bbc.co.uk/. The BBC and CNN (http://www.cnn.com) are two organizations that, at the time of this writing, allowed you to search for and retrieve the full text of past stories without a fee. You can access stories from National Public Radio at http://www.npr.org. Many local TV stations publish their web site addresses on the screen during news broadcasts. You can visit these sites directly to gain up-to-the-minute information about your community. You can use search tools to locate TV and radio station web sites or use an index such as the one at http://www.newspapers.com (**TV-Radio** or **Search** link).

# Homework

Many sites on the Internet provide help for school-related research. Some good examples are http://www.infoplease.com and http://www.discovery.com, shown in Figure 2 (click the **Discovery School** and **Homework Help** links). Or try Microsoft® Encarta® (click the **Homework** link) or http://www.studyweb.com.

**Science.** Need to understand how a toaster or a DSL modem works? The award-winning http://www.howstuffworks.com explains everything from batteries to space stations. If you need help with a science question, you can get a personal response from a scientist at sites like http://www.madsci.org (**Ask-A-Scientist** link). The Education Index (http://www.educationindex.com) offers links to some of the best science sites on the web. DiscoverySchool.com's **A-to-Z Science** offers a wide range of information. You can also visit web sites for respected science magazines like *Scientific American* at http://www.sciam.com.

Figure 2  DiscoverySchool.com

**Math.** A helpful math web site is http://school.discovery.com/homeworkhelp/webmath/. This site gives you not only answers, but clear explanations of how to arrive at the answers, so you can do it yourself next time. Have a specific math question? Ask Dr. Math at http://www.mathforum.com (**Ask Dr. Math** link). Try the **Student Center** at this site, too. Other information-packed math web sites include http://www.coolmath.com, http://www.funbrain.com, and http://www.allmath.com.

**English.** There are several good English grammar sites on the web. One is the Grammar Handbook at the Writers' Workshop of the University of Illinois at Urbana-Champaign (http://www.english.uiuc.edu/cws/wworkshop/grammarmenu.htm). For down-to-earth help with writing, try the Online Writing Lab at Purdue University (http://owl.english.purdue.edu/). For a readable, commonsense guide to style, you can't beat the classic *Elements of Style* by William Strunk, Jr., available online, along with other good books, at http://www.bartleby.com. Writing a report? Try http://www.researchpaper.com.

**Social Studies.** You can get up-to-date information about countries around the world from *The World Factbook* (CIA) at http://www. odci.gov/cia/publications/factbook (Figure 3). Current news events can be explored at the **Learning Network** at *The New York Times*. Are you interested in American history? Check out *The Web of Time* at http://www.theweboftime.com. And be sure to visit the web site for the prestigious *National Geographic* magazine at http://www.nationalgeographic.com.

**Experts and Tutors.** The Internet gives you access to experts and tutors in every subject area. You may even be able to chat online with an expert (chatting will be discussed in Lesson 4). You can e-mail a reporter about a story, interview an award-winning scientist, or have a discussion with a Nobel laureate.

**Try It!** For the odd research question, you can try simply asking it in a search tool, using the search strategies you learned in Lesson 1. It's amazing how often this works. If your first search doesn't yield the results you want, try other search terms or a different search tool (search tools index sites differently).

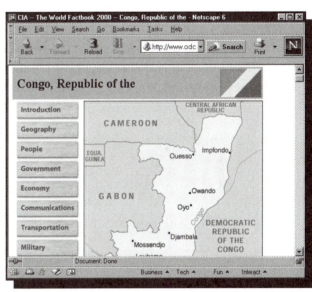

Figure 3 *The World Factbook 2000*

# Doing Personal Research on the Internet

Many people use the Internet to conduct personal research to help them in their everyday lives. You might research the weather for the weekend before you plan your trip to the beach. You might research the fair market value of your car before you trade it in. Whatever your personal research needs, the Internet can probably satisfy them.

**Education.** You can use the Internet to research colleges and other educational opportunities, as well as financial aid. You might begin at http://www.petersons.com (Figure 4) or http://www.usnews.com (click the **Education** link). Many colleges have web sites at which you can take a virtual tour of the campus, request information, ask questions, and even apply online. You will learn about online education in Lesson 6.

**Figure 4 Peterson's Web Site**

**Jobs.** The Internet is a valuable tool for job hunters. For information about different types of jobs, requirements, projected job growth, and pay, you might start at the *Occupational Outlook Handbook* online at http://stats.bls.gov/ocohome.htm. The employment or careers link at a categorical index will yield a wealth of job-getting sites with information on writing resumes, job search strategies, jobs to apply for online, interview tips, etc. You can visit general sites such as http://www.jobweb.com or specific job posting sites such as http://www.monster.com, where you can check for jobs and salary ranges and post an online resume. You can check local newspaper help-wanted ads online as well.

**Financial Information.** Many individuals do financial research. This can include everything from researching certificate of deposit (CD) rates and checking account balances to researching stocks and buying securities. All types of financial information can be found on the Internet. Yahoo!® (http://www.yahoo.com; click **Finance**), for example, provides volumes of financial information. Another excellent financial site is http://www.fool.com. You'll learn about online investing and money management in Lesson 9.

**Citizenship.** At http://www.vote-smart.org, you can research your elected representatives' personal and professional backgrounds, positions on issues, voting records, sources of campaign funding, etc. THOMAS (http://thomas.loc.gov/) has the *Congressional Record* and full text of legislation available from 1989 (101st Congress) to the present. In addition, THOMAS has summaries of legislation available back to 1975.

**Smart Buying.** Suppose you are planning to buy a used car. You want to read up on reliable models, what to look for, and what to pay. The Internet is the place for this kind of research. You might start at http://www.edmunds.com or http://www.kbb.com. Need some advice on insurance? Try http://www.smartmoney.com, http://www.kiplinger.com, or http://www.insure.com. Need to figure loan payments? Try an online calculator at http://www.kiplinger.com/tools/. Or suppose you're buying a mountain bike and need product reviews. Try http://www.consumersearch.com.

You could go ahead and buy your car, your insurance, your loan, or your mountain bike on the Internet. You'll learn about Internet shopping in Lesson 3.

Suppose you need to find a local car dealership or insurance agent. Don't search through your house for the phone book. Instead, look it up online. Yellow page directories are abundant on the web. BellSouth®, for example, provides the web site http://yp.bellsouth.com. You can select from categories, look alphabetically, search by ZIP Code or area code, and so on. There are online white pages for finding people as well. You will learn more about people searches in Lesson 5.

**Travel.** Travel is another very popular personal research area. The web provides wonderful tools for travelers. At sites like Mapquest (http://www.mapquest.com), you can obtain detailed driving directions and maps just by entering a street address or city and state. The Internet has everything you need to plan your next vacation, from choosing a destination to shopping for rates to making travel purchases. You'll learn more about what the Internet offers travelers in Lessons 3 and 7.

**Weather Reports.** Planning your garden, your vacation, or a business trip? Try The Weather Channel web site at http://www.weather.com.

**Medicine and Health.** Medical and health-related resources abound on the Internet. This opens a whole new realm of understanding and coping with medical issues. At medical web sites, people can research diseases and conditions, as well as medical therapies. They can take charge of their health by researching ways to lose weight, stay fit, eat right, manage stress, and prevent illness.

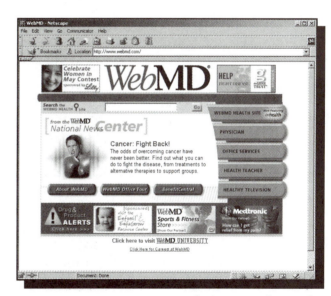

Always check on the reliability of medical web sites. Many sites run by doctors or other medical personnel provide reliable information. Give out as little personal information as possible, and read site privacy statements. Several good medical sites are http://www.webmd.com (Figure 5), http://www.mayohealth.org, and http://www.healthfinder.gov.

**Figure 5** WebMD Site

# Conclusion

The Internet can be used for all types of research. Whether you are doing school work, or personal research, the Internet has abundant information. This lesson provided an overview of many different types of information available on the Internet. Future lessons will focus more specifically on some of these resources, as well as other Internet tools.

# Activity 2-1: Do Your Homework

1. Visit http://encarta.msn.com. In the Encyclopedia tool, locate information on toucans. Access the media item linked to the text toucan information. Print the article.

2. Visit http://www.m-w.com.

   a. Find the definition of the word *plethora*.

   _____

   b. Record at least four synonyms for *plethora*.

   _____

3. Locate a local newspaper online. If you need assistance finding a local newspaper, try one of the sites mentioned in the lesson. If you do not have a local paper, access the web site of a major newspaper, such as *The New York Times*. Print a current headline news article.

4. Visit http://www.discovery.com. Find the following information on dinosaurs:

   a. What did a Parasaurolophus sound like?

   _____

   b. What did ornithischians eat?

   _____

5. Visit http://www.howstuffworks.com. Print an article on how space stations work.

6. Visit http://www.odci.gov/cia/publications/factbook. What are the main imports and exports of Belize?

   Imports: _____

   _____

   Exports: _____

   _____

7. Visit http://www.educationindex.com. Print one piece of information that can help you with your homework today.

**Research on the Net**

# Activity 2-2: Do Personal Research

1. Research the College of Culinary Arts at Johnson & Wales University in Charleston, South Carolina.

   When was it founded? _____

   How many students are enrolled? _____

   What is the tuition? _____

   Can you download an application form? _____

2. Visit http://www.monster.com. Search your area for jobs that you think you may be interested in. If you do not find any, widen your search to include other areas where you might like to work. Print at least two job postings of interest.

3. Search for the financial information needed to complete the following table:

| STOCK TICKER | LAST TRADE VALUE | 52-WEEK RANGE | VOLUME |
|:---:|:---:|:---:|:---:|
| CSCO | | | |
| MSFT | | | |
| HAS | | | |
| JNJ | | | |

4. Visit http://www.weather.com. Print a local forecast. It can be a detailed local forecast for today or a forecast for a several-day period.

5. Locate a magazine web site and find a recipe you would like to try. Print the recipe.

6. Visit http://www.vote-smart.org. Find information on one of your elected officials. Print biographical data and at least one other piece of information.

7. Use the Internet to find a place nearby where you can get a passport. Write down the address and how long it will take to get a passport. Print information on what you should bring with you to get a passport.

   _____

   _____

8. Locate a yellow pages web site. If you cannot locate another site, use http://yp.bellsouth.com. Search for a computer repair company in your area or an area close by. Write down the name and address of the company. Print a map or directions, if they are provided.

_____

## Activity 2-3: Do Research for Work

1. You need some good accounting software. Find it through an online vendor. List the vendor, the software, the price, and how long it will take to ship the software.

_____

_____

2. Find the Internal Revenue Service (IRS) web site. Write down the URL.

_____

3. Can you download federal tax forms and publications? _____

4. You are thinking of going into business for yourself. Find some information on the web about starting a small business. Print the information.

## Activity 2-4: Search Databases

1. Find five database sites. List their URLs below.

   a. _____

   b. _____

   c. _____

   d. _____

   e. _____

2. At one of these sites, locate a document that interests you, read it, and write or key a summary of it. Turn in a copy of the article with your summary.

# Activity 2-5: Plan a Trip

1. You are planning a trip to Vancouver, British Columbia for August 3 through August 15. You are thinking of taking Amtrak.

   a. Can you get to Vancouver by train from the nearest major city? _____

   b. If so, how much will a round-trip ticket cost? _____

2. If you found a way of taking the train, print your route information.

3. Maybe you will fly instead. Shop for airfares to Vancouver from the nearest major airport. Print the lowest rate and flight information.

4. Locate directions from your house to your airport. Print the directions.

5. Locate two hotels in Vancouver. Print information on rates and availability for a single room.

# Activity 2-6: Search for Medical Information

1. Go to the WebMD web site (http://www.webmd.com). Search the site for information on symptoms of gastroesophageal reflux. What are some symptoms?

   _____

   _____

   _____

2. Search for information regarding the medicine Prevacid™. Print one article that discusses how Prevacid™ is used to treat gastroesophageal reflux. Read the article and highlight important points with a pencil, pen, or highlighter.

# Activity 2-7: Do a Research Paper

Research a topic of your choice. Write a two-page research paper on your topic. Make sure you cite your resources appropriately. (If you don't know how, find out on the web!)

# 3 Shopping Online

## Focus

In 2000, consumer online purchases nearly doubled over those made in 1999, with shoppers spending some $56 billion. Consumers spent more than $6 billion online just during the 2000 holiday season, a 60 percent increase from the previous year. As of July 2000, some 27 percent of Americans had made an online purchase.

—*E-Commerce Times®, Edison Media Research*

## Overview

One Internet activity that is quickly becoming popular is the online shopping experience. Billions of dollars exchange hands across the Internet every year. More and more people are using the Internet as a primary shopping location for everything from pet food to computers. People are even using the Internet to purchase homes.

With thousands of businesses on the Internet and more coming online every day, should you buy online? This lesson will discuss the pros and cons of Internet shopping. It will show you how to find good **e-commerce** (electronic commerce) sites, how to use smart shopping tools, and how to check that a web site is reputable and that its system for processing credit card numbers and other personal information is secure.

## Finding Shopping Sites

Finding shopping sites is similar to finding any resource on the Internet. Search tools are a primary means for identifying web sites that correspond to your interests. Categorical indexes, which you learned about in Lesson 1, are often the best search tool for locating vendors. Figure 1 shows the Yahoo!® Shopping web page.

Suppose, like many Internet shoppers, you were interested in purchasing a computer system. You would select the **Computers** and then the **Desktops** link. The resulting web page provides links to several computer models and many vendors and manufacturers of computer products (Figure 2).

Figure 1 **The Yahoo!® Shopping Web Page**

If you are comparison-shopping, which many people are doing when buying online, you will visit several web sites before deciding on a vendor. One reason people use the Internet for shopping is that they hear you get the "best deals" on the Internet. This may or may not be true, depending on what you are looking for. Others may use the Internet to find a unique item they can't find in a local store.

The Internet provides you with a single interface for comparison-shopping dozens or, if you have the time, hundreds of online stores. You could spend hours searching for the best price. But you don't have to. There are comparison-shopping sites on the Internet to help you called smart shopping tools.

Figure 2 Shopping for Computers

# Smart Shopping Tools

**Smart shopping tools** are web sites, software, and web page features that help you find the products you want. One type of smart shopping tool is the comparison-shopping web site. Comparison-shopping sites integrate smart indexing technology to help you search dozens of businesses for the best price on a product.

If you are shopping for computers or computer parts, for example, you might try http://www.pricewatch.com. This site has an easy-to-use computer part index. You can make selections from the index or search for what you need. The result is a listing of parts and vendors by price (Figure 3). Many vendors have direct links to their web sites, where you can purchase the product.

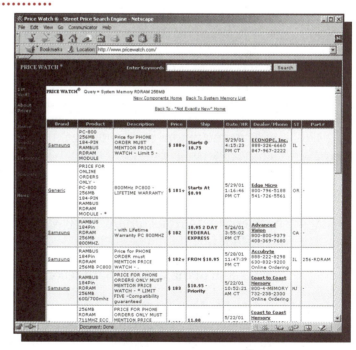

Figure 3 Price Watch® Search Results

Another example of a comparison-shopping site is http://www.mysimon.com. At mySimon, you can comparison-shop for lots of different products.

Often, you may want to research a product before you make a purchase. As you learned in Lesson 2, the web is a good resource for product reviews by both experts and consumers. One example of a product review web site is http://www.productreviewnet.com/ (PRN). In a list of 25 most useful sites, the magazine *Yahoo! Internet Life* rated PRN second. You can also get reliable product ratings for a small monthly registration fee from the respected consumer magazine *Consumer Reports*®, available online at http://www.consumerreports.org.

One complaint that consumers have about shopping on the Internet is the lack of personal service. Many e-commerce sites are addressing that concern with individualized smart shopping tools to help customers make selections. A good example is the My Virtual Model™ feature at Lands' End (http://www.lands-end.com). Using this feature, men and women can enter their height, weight, and other personal characteristics and build a model of themselves to try on clothes. This model can be saved to use again in future visits. A similar feature called My Personal Shopper suggests clothing based on shoppers' personal characteristics and preferences (Figure 4).

Figure 4 **"My Personal Shopper" at Lands' End**

Travel is one of the most popular items people shop for on the web. Travelers can save hundreds of dollars and hours of shopping time by using e-mail services. For example, suppose you are planning a trip in a few months, but the airfares right now are too high. At Travelocity.com (http://www.travelocity.com), you can use the Fare Watcher tool to specify the price you want to pay. Travelocity.com continuously monitors airfares and notifies you by e-mail when tickets become available at that price. You'll learn more about using the Internet to make travel purchases in Lesson 7.

Many online merchants use e-mail to generate future sales from their customers. For instance, shoppers at Amazon.com (http://www.amazon.com) can receive e-mail about books, movies, or music that might interest them, based on what they have purchased in the past, as well as about sales and other promotions. In addition, returning customers who log in can shop at a personalized version of the web site with recommendations geared to previous purchases.

Another smart shopping tool is the online auction. This is an online marketplace where people can post what they have for sale and others can bid on it, with the highest bidder getting the item. One of the best-known auction sites is eBay® (Figure 5). Many traditional e-commerce vendors are starting to include online auctions as a feature of their web sites. Amazon.com is a good example.

A final option that online retailers are using is the "clearance rack," where the company offers discontinued items at a discounted price. This is a great moneymaker for the company. What would normally be taken as a loss is converted to a cash sale, and someone gets a good deal!

Smart shopping tools are the wave of the future. No individual has the time to visit hundreds of e-commerce web sites looking for the lowest price. Online merchants are striving to provide individualized shopping tools that are like virtual salesclerks helping you make a selection. Smart shopping tools do it for you, are thorough, and are easy to use. These tools will likely help to increase all types of online sales.

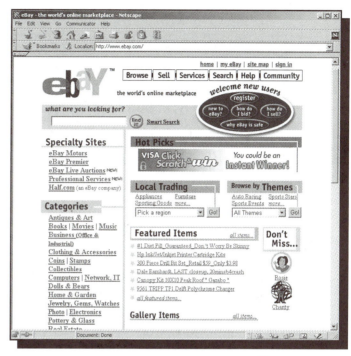

Figure 5  The eBay® Auction Site

# Where Should You Buy?

With all of these vendors and buying options, whom do you buy from? The answer depends on your personal preferences. For example, suppose you are going to purchase a computer. Do you prefer to buy from a local store, where you can take the computer back if you have any problems with it? Or is it acceptable to you to buy online, knowing that if you have a problem, you will need to ship the computer back, fix it yourself, or use a local computer repair service? Would a significant difference in price affect your decision? These are questions you have to decide for yourself.

Choosing whether to buy online may also depend on the type of product you are purchasing. You may be less likely to need to return a book or CD, and returning it may be easier. Before you make any online purchase, you should check the company's return policy, which should be provided on its web site.

Many people feel more comfortable purchasing from a name they already know. They also feel more comfortable knowing that a physical store is around the corner in case they have any problems with the purchase. These consumers may prefer to shop with a click-and-mortar vendor. A **click-and-mortar vendor** is one that has both online sales and a physical store or stores. Wal-Mart and many other large retailers fit into the category of click-and-mortar vendors, since they sell on the Internet and at physical locations. A **pure-play vendor** is one that sells only on the Internet.

If you are considering buying from a click-and-mortar vendor because you want the local support, you should know that some of these vendors do not mix their Internet and physical store location sales systems. This means that if you buy a product from the retailer's web site, you may not be able to return it to the local store. If the vendor you are planning to buy from is one of these, you may *not* get the support from the local store you expected. Make sure you research customer support and return policies on the site before you buy.

## Sales Tax and Online Buying

Most web sites do not charge sales tax if the organization does not have a physical presence in the state. This means that if the company is located, for example, in Virginia, shoppers buying from the company web site who live in Virginia will pay sales tax, but those outside of Virginia will not. Companies that do business in multiple states generally charge sales tax to people who live in the states where the company has a physical location.

Many states require you to pay tax on items you purchase online regardless of whether the company charges you sales tax. You do this on your state income tax form. You should investigate your state's tax code to determine whether you need to pay sales tax for items you buy online, particularly before making a large purchase.

Service, support, and taxes are not your only concerns when shopping online. You also need to consider the security and reliability of a web site, particularly if you are submitting a credit card number.

## Security and Reliability

Security and reliability are true concerns for shopping online. Anytime you make a purchase, whether at a physical store or on the Internet, you are susceptible to fraud. Years ago people would steal credit card carbon paper from trash cans to get peoples' credit card numbers and signatures. Today, they try to steal credit card information on the web.

Some people are fearful about using the Internet for purchases because of the cases of fraud they hear about in the news. Are these cases really any different than the stories of fraud, as mentioned above, from years ago? In most states you are only responsible, by law, for up to $50 worth of fraudulent charges anyway. As long as you have money, unscrupulous people will look for ways to take it from you. Let's look at some ways to investigate the security and reliability of a company before you submit a credit card number to it.

When you are at an e-commerce web site and are ready to submit the personal information needed to complete a sale, you should immediately look for the **encryption icon** in your browser window. The encryption symbol, a locked padlock (Figure 6), is your assurance that the information you send to the web site is only viewable by the receiving site. If you place your cursor over the padlock icon, the level of encryption being used will display. Encryption at the 128-bit level is best, but 56-bit is OK.

**Shopping Online**

To determine the security level of a web site, double-click the locked padlock symbol to get information about the company's **SSL certificate** (Figure 7). This is a certificate of authenticity and security issued to an organization by a registered certificate authority. The most widely recognized certificate authority is VeriSign®. When a company requests a certificate from VeriSign® or a similar authority, that authority conducts a series of checks to verify the organization is reliable before issuing the certificate.

Another good way to verify the reliability of a company is to check it out with the Better Business Bureau (http://www.bbb.org). For many areas of the country, this can be done online. Word of mouth is yet another excellent way to identify good Internet vendors.

Always check that contact information is *clearly* listed on an e-commerce site. If a company's site doesn't give you its business location and contact information such as e-mail addresses and phone numbers, you should question that company's reliability.

Figure 6  An Encryption Icon

Figure 7  SSL Certificate Details

# Conclusion

Internet shopping is growing by leaps and bounds. Traditional retailers are developing e-commerce sites daily, while start-up pure-play retailers are also joining the list of Internet vendors. You can use search tools and smart shopping tools to find the products and the prices you want. Before you buy, check on return and customer support policies, and be sure they are acceptable to you. Remember that Internet shopping is as safe as in-person shopping as long as you check on the reliability of the company and its security system before submitting personal information.

# Activity 3-1: Buy Online

1.  Place a check mark before each item that you know or can determine is sold online.

    _____ Automobiles    _____ Groceries    _____ Sporting goods

    _____ Furniture      _____ Insurance    _____ Stock

2.  List two products or services not discussed in this lesson that you know or can determine are sold on the World Wide Web.

    a. _____    b. _____

3.  List two products or services that you would consider buying online.

    a. _____    b. _____

4.  List two products or services that you would *not* consider buying online.

    a. _____    b. _____

5.  Why wouldn't you buy these products or services online?

    _____

6.  What are one or two advantages of shopping on the Internet?

    a. _____    b. _____

7.  What are one or two disadvantages of shopping on the Internet?

    a. _____    b. _____

# Activity 3-2: Use Smart Shopping Tools

1.  Choose a product that you would like to buy. Use a consumer research web site to research that product. Print one review.

2.  Price the product at a price comparison web site. Create a spreadsheet or table of at least three vendors and their prices. Include shipping and any other charges. Also include other factors, such as return policies, that could affect your purchase decision.

3.  Try one of the other smart shopping tools described in this lesson. Write an e-mail to your instructor describing your experience with this tool.

# Activity 3-3: Explore eBay®

1.  Visit the eBay® web auction site (http://www.ebay.com). Browse the site and look at some of the items available for purchase. Print information on two items that interest you.

2.  Find and print basic information on how to sell items on eBay®.

3.  Explore the eBay® web site. Find two tools that the site provides that you think would be helpful to buyers or sellers. List each tool and write a paragraph about it.

# Activity 3-4: Go Shopping

1.  Find a vendor and a price for the following items:

    a.  A round-trip airline ticket to a place you'd like to go

        Destination: _____

        Vendor: _____ Price: _____

    b.  A piece of clothing you'd like to buy ($75 limit)

        Vendor: _____ Price: _____

    c.  A book, CD, video, or DVD you'd like to buy ($50 limit)

        Vendor: _____ Price: _____

2.  Assume you have $200 to spend online. What would you buy, where would you buy it, and why would you buy it there? Key one or two paragraphs in a word processing file answering these questions.

# Activity 3-5: Check Security

Visit a vendor of your choice. Initiate the purchase of a product but DO NOT enter any person information. Watch the browser padlock. When it converts to a locked padlock, double-click it. Record the following information:

Certificate issued to: _____

Certificate issued by: _____

Valid from _____ to _____
                         (date)                                (date)

# 4 Using the Internet for Communications

## Focus

Human beings are human beings. They say what they want, don't they? They used to say it across the fence while they were hanging wash. Now they just say it on the Internet.

—Dennis Miller

## Overview

The Internet has been around for years. One of the early purposes for the Internet was to develop a communications system. Communications tools are therefore one of the largest segments of the Internet and Internet traffic.

**Electronic mail (e-mail),** or mail sent from computer to computer, is the most popular means of communicating on the Internet, with some 94 percent of Americans who have Internet access using it at least once a month. In 1999, by one estimate, Americans were sending about 2.1 billion e-mails each day. Speed, convenience, and low cost combine to make e-mail a favorite communications tool.

In addition to e-mail, we now have tools that allow us to send text messages and talk on the Internet in real time. **Real-time** communication means an environment in which, when you enter a message, the receiving party sees or hears it immediately. **Internet Relay Chat,** or IRC, allows users to log in to a **chat room** or online discussion where people exchange written messages in real time.

Another blooming technology is **instant messaging tools,** such as Yahoo!® Messenger, ICQ ("I Seek You"), and AOL Instant Messenger. This technology is similar to a real-time chat session but is more personalized. As soon as you connect, your computer sends a message to everyone in your contact list letting him or her know you are online. You can now chat in a real-time and personal setting.

Still another growing technology is **Voice over IP,** or Internet phone. Voice over IP allows you to call either a remote computer or a regular telephone with your computer. You talk into your computer microphone, and the receiving party hears you and can respond via his or her microphone or telephone. The connection is not usually as clear as a regular telephone connection and may include a small delay, but for a technology that is mostly *free,* what do you want? Let's examine each of these Internet communications tools in more depth.

# E-mail

E-mail is notably the most commonly used communications tool today. It is quick. Delivery usually takes place in seconds, whether the recipient is across the street or across the world. It is convenient. E-mail has virtually eliminated the problem of "phone tag." It is also inexpensive—free, in fact, with Internet access.

**Getting E-mail.** There are a number of ways that you can get an e-mail account. When you obtain an Internet service provider (ISP) to access the Internet, e-mail services are included. The software needed to access your e-mail will also be provided or may already be installed on your computer system. Another way to obtain an e-mail account is to get a free account from a provider on the Internet. Many search tools, such as Yahoo!® and Excite, allow you to register for a free e-mail account. These accounts will also usually provide you with instant messaging features and more. It is not uncommon today for people to have multiple e-mail accounts.

There are two main types of e-mail systems. One type stores the e-mail messages temporarily on the server. When you check e-mail, the messages are moved from the server to your computer hard drive. The second type stores the e-mail messages on the server. When you access the messages, they are not moved to your computer; you only view them on the server. This allows you to access your e-mail account from many different locations and still be able to view your messages, because they are stored on the server until you delete them.

Most e-mail servers require you to have e-mail software, such as Microsoft® Outlook® Express or Novell® GroupWise®, to read and send e-mail messages. However, web-based e-mail systems only require you to have a browser to access e-mail accounts.

If you want a web-based e-mail account, visit a provider such as Yahoo!® Mail (http://www.yahoo.com) or the MSN Hotmail® (http://www.hotmail.com) web-based e-mail service. Figure 1 shows a Yahoo!® Mail free e-mail account. Many people recommend this type of e-mail account because it can always go with you. If you change ISPs, you lose your old ISP e-mail account, but your free Internet account is not affected.

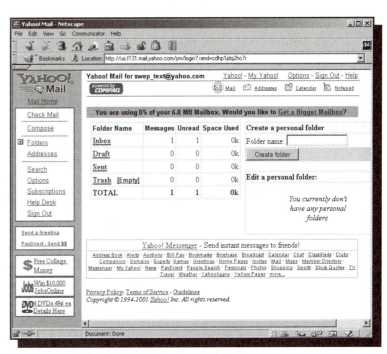

Figure 1 Yahoo!® Mail Free E-mail Account

**Writing E-mail.** E-mail messages are generally brief and more casual than letters or memos. They are quick and easy to send. These qualities can be disadvantages, however. People are sometimes less careful in writing e-mail than in writing other correspondence. And once you click **Send,** e-mail can't be taken back.

Here are a few ways that you can avoid mistakes in sending e-mail: Always read your message carefully one last time before sending it. Don't use e-mail when a telephone call or face-to-face meeting would be better; for instance, if you have bad news to deliver. Be considerate of your reader's time by being brief and to the point. Make sure you provide enough background information so the recipient knows what your message is about.

**E-mail Features.** Features are generally the same across e-mail systems. There is usually an address book in which you can store frequently used e-mail addresses. You can insert these addresses into e-mail automatically, which saves time and prevents keying errors. There are also features for sending copies and forwarding e-mail to others.

The **Reply** feature is an efficient way of responding to a message. This feature inserts the recipient's address and the subject line for you. It also quotes the original message automatically, leaving space for your response.

Electronic mail allows you to send not only messages but also documents or computer files of any type. This is referred to as sending **attachments.** An attachment can be any computer file—a word processing file, a graphic, a ZIP file, and so on. This textbook was written and edited using this technology.

But beware. Many computer viruses are sent as e-mail attachments. If you open one of these attachments, the virus can enter your computer system and damage it. Watch or read the news to find out about new viruses, and don't open e-mail messages from unfamiliar sources or attachments you were not expecting. Anyone using the Internet should have up-to-date virus protection software, which we will cover in Lesson 10.

Now that we have discussed e-mail, which is not real-time, what else is available? What if I need to talk to someone now, real-time, and I don't have time to wait for an e-mail message? How about IRC?

# Internet Relay Chat (IRC)

Internet Relay Chat, or just Chat, has been around for a number of years. It began as a globally distributed real-time discussion forum. You could log in to a local IRC server, find a chat room based on an area of interest or set up your own, and begin a text-based discussion with other people in the chat room. A chat room is a virtual room that has a subject name, such as *Herbs_room*, where I could tell friends to log in and meet me so we could talk online (by text messages). IRC servers host thousands of chat rooms that are replicated globally so that your chat room and discussion are open to people around the world.

**Using the Internet for Communications**

IRC also has a web-based form that is usually specific to just one server. For example, you might visit http://www.talkcity.com and join a chat room or make your own. However, someone wanting to meet you in your chat room would also have to log in to Talk City to find your chat room—it is not replicated globally.

IRC systems have evolved beyond simple text-only environments to locations where files can be exchanged between participants and even small sound clips can be heard. Figure 2 shows the screen after a login to the Talk City web site. The new window that appears is the chat interface that you will use to "talk" to others and join in discussion in the various chat rooms.

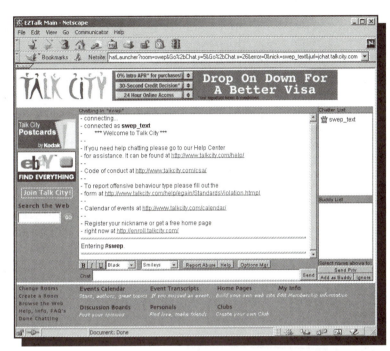

Figure 2  Talk City Chat Interface

Chat is a good technology for real-time communications, but it does require you to know which chat room your friends will be in so that you can meet them.

## Instant Messaging

A new technology emerged from the IRC tools to allow you to skip the chat-room concept but keep the real-time personal communications model. Instant messaging tools are that technology. Once you install an instant messaging tool and connect to a messaging server, you can communicate with others who have the same instant messaging system through a small chat window. Figure 3 shows a Yahoo!® Messenger interface allowing for chat communications.

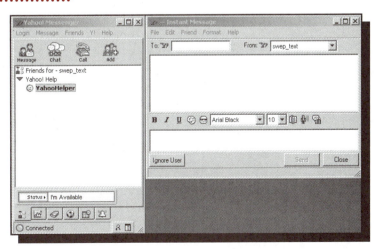

Figure 3  Yahoo!® Messenger Interface

Instant messaging software allows you to specify other user accounts to which you would like to be connected. For example, you might specify the accounts for your parents, your friends, and maybe even your grandmother. As soon as you connect, any of the other people whom you specified who are currently online see that you too are now online and can start chatting with you. Notice that this technology does not require you to log in to a specific chat room, only to connect and start communicating.

Instant messaging is rapidly becoming the communications tool of choice for the younger generation. Friends can communicate at any time as long as they are connected to the Internet, have the same messaging system, and have specified each other's accounts.

Instant messaging and IRC technologies are great real-time communications tools. Instant messaging is also expanding to allow you to communicate by talking through your computer microphone to someone else's computer on the other end. The person located at the receiving computer hears your voice through his or her computer speakers. Still, this technology is not the same as talking to someone on the phone. Well, it just so happens that someone has thought of a way to talk across the Internet from a computer to a standard telephone.

## Voice Over IP (Internet Phone)

**Voice over IP** (Internet Protocol) or Internet phone technologies are rapidly increasing in use. Originally the Internet was not considered a good pathway for voice traffic because of the packet-switching technology employed by the Internet for routing traffic. Regular telephone traffic is carried across a line in a single signal from one telephone to another. The Internet, however, breaks each communication into multiple chunks called packets that are sent across the Internet via different paths. At the receiving site the packets, or pieces, are reassembled into the original format. The delay that occurs in breaking content into packets and reassembling is not evident when you visit a web site but is very obvious with voice communications. However, with recent advancements in Voice over IP technologies, the Internet is starting to carry more voice traffic with higher quality than before. The technology will only continue to improve over the next several years. For those users with high-speed Internet connections (higher than 56K), the technology already works well.

To use this technology, you must have a computer with a sound card, a microphone, and either headphones or speakers. A headset with headphones and a microphone are the ideal hardware for this type of communication. The software required to make an Internet phone call may be purchased or downloaded and may use your browser as the interface for making the call.

Using this technology, you can call from your computer to another computer or a regular telephone. Yes, you can call from your computer, across the Internet, and your friend picks up a regular telephone receiver and he or she talks to you! Figure 4 shows the telephone interface for http://www.net2phone.com, where you can call a regular phone line with your computer.

This technology is being used in virtual schools for instructors to talk with students (we will look at online learning in Lesson 6). Some organizations are also using VoIP for communications between branch offices and headquarters over existing wide area network connections (computer networks that cover a large geographic area). This technology will continue to improve and become more widely available.

**Figure 4** Net2Phone Client Application

## Privacy and Security

Now let's talk about privacy and security issues with some of these communications technologies.

E-mail is not private. Even messages that have been deleted can be saved in company computers, and courts have supported employers' rights to read their employees' e-mail messages. Employees have been fired for including in e-mail sensitive, illegal, or unethical information. A good rule of thumb is to avoid putting anything in an e-mail that you would not want to see posted on a bulletin board at school or work.

IRC discussions are also not private. Since you use a nickname or handle when chatting, your identity isn't known (except to the IRC if you entered personal information when registering), but your communications can be viewed by anyone. Further details regarding privacy and security with IRC will be addressed in Lesson 5.

You are NEVER anonymous on the Internet. The Internet uses IP addresses to communicate. These are numerical addresses that identify computers on the Internet. Each IP address is unique; no two computers can use the same address. If you are in a computer lab, the computer you are working on has a specific IP address that can be tracked. This is one way that investigators can quickly track down an individual computer that sent out a virus across the Internet—as you have likely seen on the news. If you are connecting to the Internet through an ISP, you are still assigned an IP address as long as you are logged in to the ISP computer system.

Don't worry! This does not mean that someone can find you and your home address with a computer IP address. This only means that authorities can identify where something originated if they need to track it down.

## Conclusion

As you can see, communications across the Internet come in many forms. The older e-mail and IRC tools are still used extensively for communications. However, newer technologies are quickly becoming more popular and will only continue to grow and improve. For many people, the Internet is now the primary means of daily communication.

## Activity 4-1: Use Web-Based E-mail

1. Log in to the free Internet e-mail provider web address supplied by your instructor. Read and print the rules for use of e-mail accounts.

2. Create a new e-mail account. Write down your new e-mail address.

   _____

3. E-mail your instructor from your new address. Write one or two paragraphs on your opinion of whether organizations (and schools) should have the right to view any employee's (or student's) e-mail that is stored on their computer systems. Use a brief, specific subject line. Follow the guidelines for writing e-mail given in this lesson.

## Activity 4-2: Send an Attachment

1. Search the Internet and find a current news story (not older than one year) about an e-mail virus. Read the article and print it.

2. Key a several-paragraph summary of the article, including one paragraph on how you would protect yourself from this threat, in word processing software. Save the file.

3. Find out how to send e-mail attachments in your software. Document the steps below.

   _____

   _____

   _____

   _____

   _____

   _____

   _____

   _____

4. E-mail your summary to your instructor as an attachment. Compose a cover e-mail message.  Follow the guidelines for writing e-mail given in this lesson.

**Using the Internet for Communications**

## Activity 4-3: Join a Chat Room

1. Visit http://www.talkcity.com and select the **Join now!** link. Read the **Your Right to Privacy** information.

2. Visit the **Help** link and skim through the infomation under the subheading "All About Chat."

3. With your instructor's permission, create for yourself an account and nickname. Supply only the required personal information.

4. Enter Talk City. Once the chat applet has loaded, using your instructor's directions, log in to the chat room that your instructor has set up.

5. Discuss with your fellow students the following topics:

   a. What information did you find out in Activity 4-2?

   b. Have you used instant messaging technology? If so, for how long? What do you think of it?

   c. What sort of Internet communication do you think you will use (or would like to see) in the future?

## Activity 4-4: Chat with Yahoo!® Messenger

1. Go to http://www.yahoo.com and select the link for **Yahoo!® Messenger.** Print and read the directions for downloading the messenger software for your computer platform.

2. With your instructor's permission, download and install the Yahoo!® Messenger software. Be sure to read the terms of service before accepting them.

3. Create a new account and select a login name or handle. (**Note:** If you created a Yahoo! e-mail account in Activity 4-1, use the same ID and password for Yahoo!® Messenger; you do not need to create new ones.)

4. Form a group of three or four people. Log in individually to the service and select your fellow group members to be in your immediate connection list. Once you connect, you should see the others connect. Use the software to hold a discussion on the topic provided by your instructor.

# 5 Community on the Internet

## Focus

Write a sentence defining the word *community*. Write a paragraph describing your community.

## Overview

As you have read, the Internet has become a primary communications tool for many people. In the process, it has given rise to new types of communities where people can gather and share ideas and information. The Internet has become more than just a communications medium. It has become a world of communities, like the town or county you live in.

People find new friends online, and some have even found wives or husbands. These friends may have met in person, but many times they have never seen one another and may never see each other. Individuals may come together with mutual interests or the opposite: they may enjoy debating their different opinions.

The Internet has also become a means for improving or rebuilding relationships in the real world. Tools like e-mail and family web pages help relatives keep in touch and become closer. People search tools reunite long-lost friends, classmates, and veterans who served together in the military.

Individuals are not the only people building these communities. Businesses see online communities as a way to increase sales and reach customers who may be interested in their products. Professional, social, and political groups build virtual communities to attract and unify members and further goals.

Regardless of the purpose for building an online community, it is Internet communications tools that make it possible. This lesson will introduce some new tools and will take another look at some familiar tools that are being used in this way.

## Chat Groups

Internet Relay Chat, as discussed in Lesson 4, is a primary tool for creating and fostering online communities and individual relationships. You may find a specific chat room that you are interested in and regularly visit that chat room. In those regular visits you meet others and begin to remember their login names. Before long you are discussing world politics, the latest rock band, or the coolest video game that just hit the market. You feel like you are a part of a family.

Chat communities can be based on almost any topic or area. Many chats rooms are formed by people in the same age group, school, and so on. Others may be formed around topical issues or common interests such as reading, music, hobbies, sports, games, cars, and travel, to name just a few. Many organizations are beginning to use chat to communicate with a population or community as a whole. Online virtual town meetings may be conducted in chat rooms to discuss current issues. The most popular chats, however, may be with famous people. Many chats now allow you to "talk" online with favorite rock stars about their latest album releases or with actors or actresses about their newest movies.

These communities of chat groups seem to just flourish. Some Internet service providers offer hundreds of chat rooms for discussions. Some of these providers monitor their chat rooms, or a certain list of chat rooms, for inappropriate behavior and will take action if required. These are referred to as **moderated** chat rooms—rooms that are supervised by a neutral party. Figure 1 shows a chat room. Chat rooms that are not moderated should be used with caution. Chat rooms are just one way to foster the feeling of community on the Internet.

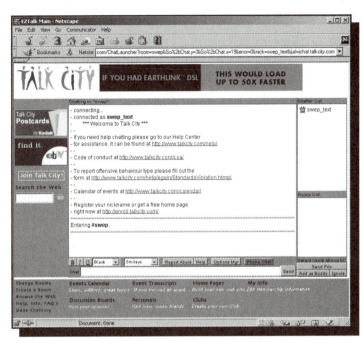

Figure 1  Chat Room at Talk City

# Web-Based Discussion Forums

Yet another tool for building online communities is the web-based discussion forum. Web forums, also referred to as newsgroups, bulletin boards, discussion groups, and threaded discussions, provide a way for individuals to leave messages for one another electronically. These messages are "posted" or stored on a computer system where people can visit a web site, read the messages that interest them, and leave replies if desired.

This technology is different from chat is one major respect: it is not real-time. Messages are composed and left in a central location. These messages are not seen until someone goes to the site with their browser and views them. Visitors must return regularly to check the discussion forum to see if anyone has responded to their posted messages. This can be an advantage because you can view the messages at your leisure and not immediately, as is required in a real-time environment like chat. Because this technology is not real-time, and people are not trying to key fast to keep up with the discussion, you will often get longer and more thoughtful postings in a web-based discussion group.

Like chat, web discussion forums are usually centered about a common theme or interest. Many of the same interest areas mentioned in the section on chat are also web discussion topic areas. Online communities use these discussion boards to share experiences, knowledge, and thoughts. Let's assume I like to take backpacking trips around the United States. I locate an

online discussion forum that specializes in backpack trip travel. I begin to tell my backpacking stories on the discussion forum and find many other people have similar stories to tell. I am planning a trip to the Grand Teton Mountains, and I post a message asking if anyone has made a similar trip. I check back in a few days and find several responses, including one from Jeanne who has written to me about where she went, what she saw, and the things she would have done differently. After reading peoples' responses, I am able to plan a wonderful trip, and I know what not to do.

If this were a threaded discussion, my question about my upcoming trip would be listed with other original messages. The respondents' messages (replies to my question) would be indented in the list of messages under my original and linked together. Non-threaded discussion forums are usually harder to navigate because all messages fall under one level and are not linked (threaded) together.

# E-mail

E-mail is a powerful tool for bringing people together. It enables family members and friends who are far away from one another—or not so far away but not always able to meet—to communicate easily, inexpensively and, as a result, more often. A recent survey found that 64 million Americans use e-mail to communicate with family members. Fifty-nine percent of those surveyed said that e-mail kept them more in touch with their relatives.

Organizations have long used newsletters to keep individuals up to date on current happenings. Today, many businesses distribute newsletter-style e-mails to people based on their interests. By doing this, these companies are attempting to build a community of individuals with the same interests to whom they can market their products and services.

The magazine *InfoWorld*®, for example, offers many e-mail newsletters to which you can subscribe online. These newsletters cover subjects such as wireless technology or e-commerce. They are delivered to your e-mail account twice a day, daily, or weekly, depending on the newsletter.

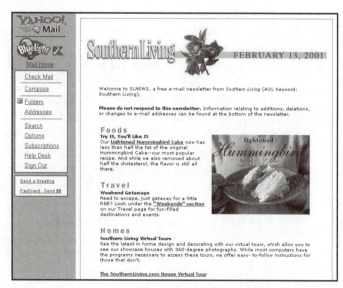

*Southern Living* magazine regularly sends an e-mail to my account showing me highlights from their magazine (Figure 2). It really grabs my attention, especially the free recipes. Many of the resources the magazine provides in its e-mails are free; however, some items require a purchase. Notice the layout of the message; it looks like a magazine

Figure 2  Web-enhanced E-mail

cover. This is a **web-enhanced** e-mail message. Most e-mail messages are text-only messages; however, web-enhanced messages are formatted as web pages and can display text, graphics, and more. These messages are basically web pages that are sent through e-mail.

Online vendors are also trying to establish virtual communities of loyal customers through personal service. As you learned in Lesson 3, many sites provide you with e-mails about sales and other promotions, products that might interest you, and special events to get your attention and your business.

Politicians, political parties, and special interest groups have discovered the value of e-mail in building communities of supporters. Political campaigns use e-mail to mobilize followers and to respond rapidly to campaign developments. Officeholders send newsletters by e-mail to constituents. Special interest groups e-mail members when an important issue arises, encouraging them to send e-mails in response. Some organizations' web sites provide links to e-mail addresses of political officials and even give visitors advice on how to write their e-mails.

E-mail makes it easier perhaps than it has ever been before for you to build or join a community to support the people and causes you believe in. Take, for example, the efforts of Jody Williams. She spent much of a year sending e-mails from her Vermont farmhouse to convince countries to ban anti-personnel landmines, which have been estimated to kill or maim someone—often a farmer or a child—every 20 minutes. Her International Campaign to Ban Landmines (ICBL) began with just three people.

Just six years later, more than 120 nations signed a treaty pledging to stop making these mines, to destroy stockpiles within four years, and to remove deployed mines within ten. ICBL's role in securing the treaty was so important that, with Williams, it won the Nobel Peace Prize. E-mail played a vital role in the effort's success.

# Finding People

The Internet provides some useful tools for finding friends, relatives, classmates, and other people with whom we have lost contact. For example, the web site http://www.classmates.com maintains databases of high school graduates and veterans that you can search. This is partially a pay service. Many Internet tools offer free basic searches, but you may have to pay for more detailed or specialized information.

Many of the major search engines have links to a people search tool. There are also independent sites devoted to these types of searches. People search tools allow you to search telephone and e-mail directories and other types of databases. These searches may yield street addresses, phone numbers, e-mail addresses, personal web pages, and other information. To conduct a search, you usually need, besides a name, some piece of information such as a state of residence.

People search engines are only as good as the currency of their database records. I have used several of these systems and have found my address and phone number—but from several years ago and therefore out of date. You are unlikely to find entries for people who have unlisted

phone numbers. Figure 3 shows the search interface for the Yahoo!® people search tool (http://people.yahoo.com).

Web sites for schools and professional organizations are good free resources. Surprisingly, even a simple query in a search engine like Google™ (*Beverly High School Alumni 1976*) can sometimes help you find someone.

## Clubs

Communities are also built around people with similar interests. Think about what you like to do. Is it skiing? Is it biking? Is it playing video games? Regardless of your interests, there are likely groups somewhere devoted to those same interests. Do you like to kayak? If so, you will find that there are dozens of groups devoted to just that sport.

Categorical indexes can often be the easiest way to find some of the more common types of groups. If you are interested in crafts, for example, you can look under **Clubs** or a similar link in a categorical index such as Yahoo! (http://www.yahoo.com) or Search.com (http://www.search.com). Figure 4 shows a categorical listing of different crafts. Clicking one of these items, such as **Basketry,** will yield a list of clubs devoted to that craft. You can also use search engines, meta search engines, or word of mouth to locate clubs in areas that interest you.

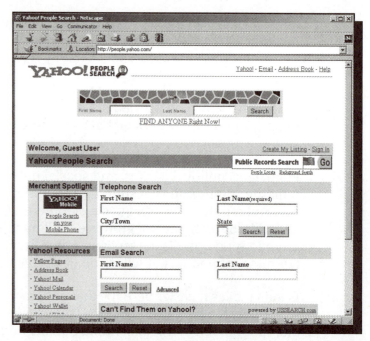

Figure 3 The Yahoo!® People Search Tool

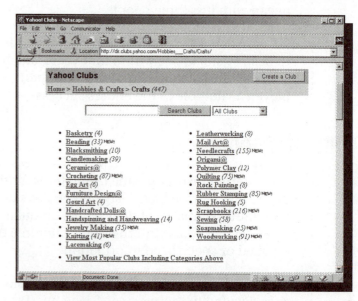

Figure 4 Crafts Clubs Categories at Yahoo!®

Many of these clubs provide communications tools as well as links to related sites. Instant messaging, chat, and web-based discussion forums allow interested individuals to share their thoughts and knowledge. For example, suppose I am learning how to weave baskets. I have completed all but the top fringe of a basket, but I don't know how to finish the top edge. I find a club for beginning basket weavers and post a message in the discussion forum for help on finishing my basket. I check back a couple of days later and find a response from a community member with a web address to a site that shows me step-by-step how to finish my basket. What a wonderful tool clubs can be!

## Online Etiquette and Safety

You need to be aware that not everyone on the Internet is a reputable person. There are predators. Therefore, when you use any of the Internet tools discussed in this lesson to communicate online, never give out information that may be used to identify you personally. This includes your name, where you live (even the region of the country), the school you attend, your age, your phone number, your mailing address, and even the mascot of your school. Sharing some of this information might seem harmless, but an unscrupulous person could use it to identify you. In addition, always check the privacy policy of a web site before using its communication tools. USE YOUR HEAD!

When communicating online, you should conduct yourself using proper etiquette or, in the online community—**netiquette**. Netiquette refers to etiquette in online environments. Netiquette includes not using all caps in your messages (this is considered shouting), not sending mass e-mails to everyone in an e-mail list (just send to those who need the message), and refraining from flaming, which is sending rude and derogatory messages. Many web sites, particularly those hosted by ISPs, provide links to basic netiquette rules. Netiquette includes many of the same rules that you may have heard: be nice to others, respect others, be courteous, etc. Most etiquette rules that apply to the physical world apply to the virtual world!

## Conclusion

The reach of the Internet and the communications tools that are available on the Internet are helping to develop extensive online communities and to build or rebuild relationships in the real world. As technologies improve and more people get online, these communities will continue to flourish and grow into larger and more diverse organizations. For centuries the coffeehouse has been a meeting place. The diner was once, too. Now the Internet serves as the location for people to gather, share ideas, and build a sense of community.

# Activity 5-1: Join a Chat or Discussion Forum

1. Visit one of these sites or another with your instructor's approval. Under the supervision of your instructor, find a chat room or forum that interests you.

   ■ Talk City at http://www.talkcity.com (select the **Chat** link)

   ■ Yahoo!® at http://www.yahoo.com (select the **Clubs** link, find a club that interests you, and locate the discussion forum link, which is called **Messages**)

2. Follow the conversation for a while, or read the postings. Are there leaders and people who dominate the conversation? Are the comments friendly, combative, lively, quiet, and so on? How are newcomers treated? Do there seem to be rules? Take notes on points like these.

3. With your instructor's permission, join the chat or post a message. How do the others respond to you? Take some notes on your experience.

4. Use your notes to compose a few paragraphs describing the community.

# Activity 5-2: Subscribe to an E-mail Service

1. Search the Internet for an organization that interests you that offers free e-mail updates or news. Read any statements at the site on privacy and use of personal information.

2. With your instructor's permission, subscribe to one of these e-mail services.

3. When you get your first edition, e-mail your instructor with answers to these questions:

   a. Did you find the e-mail helpful and informative?

   b. What types of information were included?

   c. Would you like to continue receiving it?

# Activity 5-3: Use People Search Tools

1. Form a group with two other people. Each person should choose a different people search site. Several sites are listed in the Quick Reference Guide on page 89.

2. Search for the following names and locations. In each instance, record the number of listings you got. Print your results for *A. Smith*.

| NAME | LOCATION | NO. OF HITS |
|------|----------|-------------|
| A. Smith | Washington, D.C. | |
| Mary Jones | Atlanta, GA | |
| Tony Washington | Chicago, IL | |
| Tammy Simpson | Boston, MA | |
| Your name | Your city and state | |
| B* Liang | New York, NY | |

The asterisk (*) is a wild card character meaning any name starting with a *B*. In many people search tools, the asterisk wild card will work. If you find that searching with an asterisk does not yield different names beginning with *B,* check the help feature on the site to see if a wild card is available and how to enter one. If a wild card is not an option, omit this name.

3. After you have finished searching, compare results with your group members and answer the following questions:

   a. Did you find listings for all the names? _____

   b. Did you get the same results using all three people search tools? _____

# Activity 5-4: Visit Clubs or Other Groups

Using search tools, locate six clubs or groups in areas that interest you. Record the information requested below. Write a paragraph describing the site you like best.

| URLS | INFORMATION ONLY | CHAT ROOMS | DISCUSSION FORUMS | E-MAIL UPDATES | |
|------|------------------|------------|-------------------|----------------|--|
| 1. | | | | | |
| 2. | | | | | |
| 3. | | | | | |
| 4. | | | | | |
| 5. | | | | | |
| 6. | | | | | |

# 6 Educational Opportunities on the Net

## Focus

## Overview

It's no wonder that the Internet and World Wide Web have quickly become avenues for education and training (Figure 1). In a traditional classroom, you have an instructor who is lecturing, answering questions, and perhaps showing slides or overhead transparencies. You have a lively interchange of ideas among instructors and students. You can have all this and more in an online environment.

Educational opportunities abound on the Internet. You can visit any search engine, search for *online education* or *distance education,* and find thousands of web sites devoted to learning. Most of the pay sites belong to professional training organizations or colleges and universities. Other sites offer free online tutorials in specific areas or tasks such as web page design.

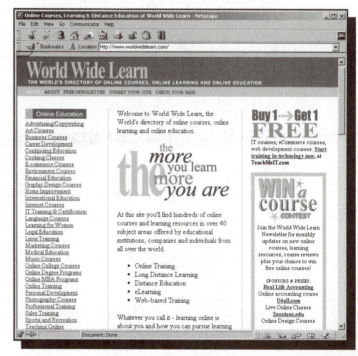

Figure 1  Directory of Online Learning

## What Is Distance Education?

What is distance education? This term has very different meanings for different people. In general, **distance education** refers to delivering educational material to a distant location. You may also see terms like **distance learning** or even **distributed learning.** Distance education can take many forms. It can include (1) satellite delivery, (2) videotaped courses, (3) correspondence (by mail) courses, (4) Internet-based courses, and more.

Today, when most people think of distance education, they are thinking of online learning environments or Internet/web-based learning. For some, a class that uses e-mail to communicate with students is an Internet-delivered course. For others, distance education may mean a complete, **synchronous** (or real-time) class on the Internet that includes audio, video, graphics, chat rooms, and more. For this discussion, we will focus on complete online courses, online degrees, and short online tutorials.

Online distance education encompasses everything from a five-minute lesson on how to sink a putt to corporate and military training to a doctoral degree in economics. It is provided by high schools, traditional colleges and universities, training organizations, and even individuals who post a web page to pass on their skills. Entire schools (or specialty schools) are now available online. The state of Virginia, for example, has a virtual Governor's School that offers gifted students advanced classes in a completely online learning environment (Figure 2).

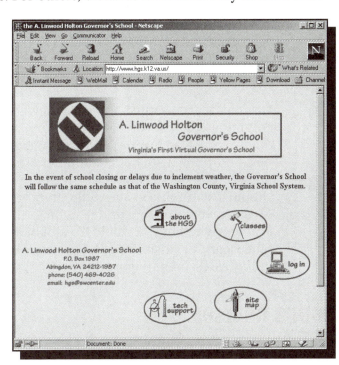

Figure 2 Virtual Governor's School

# Who Uses Distance Education?

Hundreds of thousands of people are enrolled in online learning courses—about 700,000 in 1999 alone. Many are adults in the workforce who want to earn a degree, learn new software, qualify for professional advancement, or otherwise continue their education but don't have time to attend school during the day. In many states, lawyers, nurses, and other professionals can earn continuing professional education credits online. Another group is workers required or encouraged by their employers to take online training at work on the Internet or company intranet. Still others are at-home parents or dropouts returning to school.

Some college students choose online learning because they live far away from the college they want to attend. It has become easier to do so; about 75 percent of two- and four-year colleges and universities offer some form of online education. Students enrolled in brick-and-mortar colleges may take a course online that is closed on campus or that they can't fit into their schedule. High school students use online learning to take classes for college credit or classes not offered at their school. Many people take short online tutorials to learn a new skill or for help completing a task.

# Is It for Me?

Distance learners have to be self-motivated and well organized. Since you have the freedom to learn anytime and anywhere, you have to be able to set yourself deadlines and motivate yourself to complete the work. Motivation is probably the number-one factor in determining your success in a distance education course.

Distance learners must also be somewhat computer-savvy. If you are considering an online course, for example, you should at least be comfortable with basic computer operations such as saving and opening files. You should also be able to access the Internet and do basic web browsing and searching. To help evaluate whether you would do well in a distance learning environment, you can take an online assessment (Figure 3).

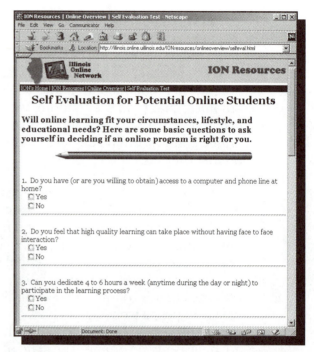

Figure 3  Online Learning Self-Assessment

# Online Courses

**Online courses** are complete courses on specific subjects that you can take using the Internet or a company intranet. Most colleges and universities offer online courses ranging from introductory computer classes to advanced chemistry and others. You can usually obtain college or high school credit for these courses. Online courses can be taken individually or as part of a complete degree program. Secondary schools are also getting into the online course market. If your high school does not offer a Latin course, but a high school across town does, you may be able to take the other school's Latin course online.

Consultants and training organizations develop online courses for businesses. Training is costly; so are the travel and lost work time associated with it. Employees can complete online courses on the Internet or corporate intranet at work, at their own pace.

Online courses are delivered using a variety of technologies, including web pages, discussions forums, and live chat sessions. They may also include audio and video components. Many of these courses are offered using special course creation and hosting software, such as Blackboard and WebCT® (Figure 4).

A lot of online courses use similar software packages and therefore look very similar. The web page in Figure 4 was created with online course software and shows the main components that you will find in most online courses. Notice you have posted Announcements (or updates), Course Information, Course Documents, a Discussion Board (for posting and reading messages),

**Educational Opportunities on the Net**

a Virtual Classroom (for chats), Assignments, External Links to helpful information, and much more. Some courses even have links to external sound clips of lectures, animations, and short video clips.

## How Does It Work?

Online learning can take many forms. Let's say you have registered for an on-line course. You receive a username, password, and Internet location. You go to the location, log in, and find yourself in the online classroom.

Here you have a set of buttons you can click. The first one takes you to the course information or syllabus. You read the syllabus, return to your "class-room," and spend some time orienting yourself to the classroom interface and what each link provides. You locate links to all course assignments, other course documents (readings, etc.), and discussion tools and chat rooms where you can collaborate with other students.

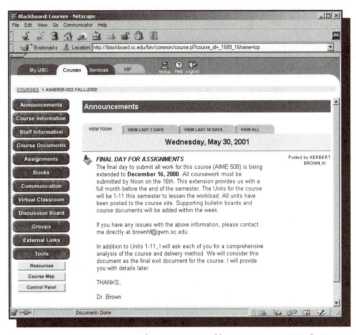

**Figure 4** Online Course Web Page

Now you begin your assignments. You post your thoughts about the assigned readings on a discussion board. A couple of days later, you visit the discussion board and see that someone else in the class has left comments for you regarding your posting. You post a response to their comments, and the online discussion begins.

You continue through the course completing assignments and e-mailing documents to your instructor. Your class lectures are slide shows posted to the class web site. You can even hear the lectures, because your instructor has recorded sound files and attached them to the slides.

Most online courses require only a computer with Internet access, a browser, and possibly free mini-applications like a media player. If special software is required, the school will either provide it or let you know what to get and where to buy it. The faster your computer and Internet access, the less likely you are to have technical problems. If you are accessing simple web documents with graphics and text, a 56K modem will be sufficient. However, if you are expected to watch video clips and listen to audio-based lectures, you should have a faster Internet connection so you will not become frustrated with the amount of time it takes to download these files.

Before you sign up for an online course, try to sit in on a sample class. See if you are comfortable with online learning and whether your computer hardware and software will work adequately. Find out if technical support is available.

# Online Degrees

Many institutions now offer college degree programs online. These include traditional two- and four-year colleges and universities, as well as institutions that exist only online. You could be anywhere in the world and complete an associate's, bachelor's, master's, or doctoral degree without ever physically attending the college or by attending only a few short sessions (known as a **residency requirement**). Figure 5 shows an index of some online degree programs.

Many online degree programs are reputable. Some, however, are fraudulent. You need to investigate online degree programs as thoroughly as you would those at brick-and-mortar institutions.

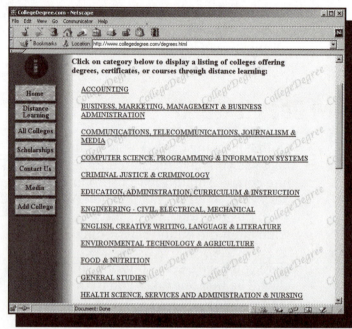

**Figure 5** Index of Online Degree Programs

- Determine whether the school is accredited and stable and has a good reputation. A good starting point for this kind of research is http://www.degree.net.

- Look at what credentials your field of work requires. Will the degree program do what you want it to—help you get a better job, earn professional advancement, and so on?

- Research the faculty.

- Ask for names and addresses of graduates who can tell you about the program.

# Online Tutorials

Online tutorials are different from online courses because they are generally shorter and teach a specific task. For example, suppose you are creating web pages and would like to add some JavaScript for scrolling text, but you don't know JavaScript. If you search the Internet, you will find a number of sites with short tutorials on how to code using JavaScript.

Many tutorials are computer-related. Others teach skills as varied as how to build a birdhouse, fix a stuck ignition, or write a song. Figure 6 shows a tutorial for learning HTML scripting.

Most online tutorials are simple to use and FREE! Yes, free. They are created by people who know their subject and want to share their knowledge. Tutorials are only as comprehensive and good as the person who created them.

If you are trying to learn a new skill or need help completing a task, search the Internet. You will probably find that someone has created a tutorial for what you need to learn. A good site to start from is http://www.about.com (at the time of this writing, choose **Education, Distance Learning,** and **Free Courses**).

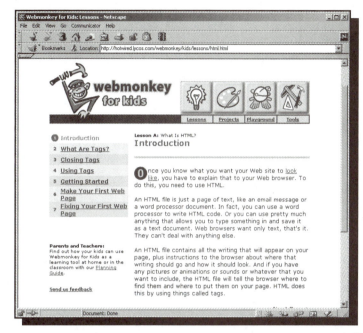

Figure 6  Online Tutorial[1]

# Pros and Cons of Online Learning

There are many advantages to online learning. The most obvious is that, in many cases, you can go to school when and where you want to. You can sit at home in your pajamas at 2 a.m. and learn. You can take one or two courses at a time and finish a degree at your own pace. Online learning fits well in a world where people seem to have more and more demands on their time. Online learning is also sometimes less expensive than classes at brick-and-mortar schools.

The online learning environment is conducive to many different learning styles and personalities. Some students prefer online learning because they feel more comfortable expressing themselves when they don't see the other people in a classroom face-to-face. Through chat rooms and discussion boards, students in distance education courses sometimes have more contact with classmates than in traditional classrooms. These tools may offer opportunities for more small-group interaction than traditional classes, particularly large lecture classes.

There are disadvantages to the online format. Some people believe it can't replicate the give-and-take of classroom discussion and the dynamics of a good lecture. They think it depersonalizes the relationship between instructor and student. Many students benefit from being part of a traditional college or university environment. If you are not self-disciplined and self-motivated, if a class is not well chosen, or if you do not have the computer equipment or expertise for it, online learning may not be right for you.

# Conclusion

Online learning is a wonderful use of the Internet. With Internet tools, people can enjoy a wealth of educational opportunities online. Online learning will not disappear anytime soon; just the opposite, it will continue to grow by leaps and bounds.

---

[1]  Copyright ©1994–2001 Wired Digital, Inc., a Lycos Network Company. All Rights Reserved.

## Activity 6-1: Take an Online Learning Self-Evaluation

Is online learning right for you? Take a self-evaluation at one of the following sites. Print your results.

- http://illinois.online.uillinois.edu/ (choose **ION Resources, Online Learning: An Overview,** and **Self Evaluation Quiz**)

- http://www.pbs.org/als/college/

## Activity 6-2: What's Your Opinion?

U.S. Supreme Court Justice Ruth Bader Ginsburg has said, "I am uneasy about classes in which students learn entirely from home, in front of a computer screen, with no face-to-face [interaction] with other students and instructors." Write an e-mail to your instructor in which you **agree** or **disagree** with this statement and give your reasons.

## Activity 6-3: Find Online Courses

Using search tools, locate six courses that you would be interested in taking. Include the cost for each course.

| | COURSE TITLE | URL | COST |
|---|---|---|---|
| 1 | | | |
| 2 | | | |
| 3 | | | |
| 4 | | | |
| 5 | | | |
| 6 | | | |

## Activity 6-4: Take a Sample Course

Some colleges, universities, and degree programs give you the opportunity to try a sample online course free. Here are a few examples:

- Global MBA Online at the University of Texas at Dallas
  http://som.utdallas.edu/globalmba/ (select **Course Structure Demo**)

- DeVry University
  http://www.devry.edu/ (select **DeVry Online**)

- Michigan State University Criminal Justice Internet Program
  http://cjms.vu.msu.edu/ (select **online demonstration**)

With a partner, find a college or university that offers a free demo course and try it, or sample a demo course at one of the universities listed above. Write a paragraph assessing your experience. Was the online course interface easy to use? Describe some features you liked or disliked. Would you be interested in taking an online course like this? Why or why not?

## Activity 6-5: Compare Online Degree Programs

Using search tools, locate three degree programs that you would be interested in pursuing. Create a spreadsheet or table that compares the programs in terms of accreditation and total cost. Include in your spreadsheet one or two other items you learned about in this lesson that would be helpful in comparing the programs.

## Activity 6-6: Locate Online Tutorials

Select one or more topics that you would like to learn more about or a task that you would like to learn how to do. Search the Internet for free online tutorials. Record the titles and URLs below. Some web sites provide an estimate of the time required to complete the tutorial. Include in your list at least one brief tutorial (5 to 20 minutes). Put a star (*) beside the title(s) of the brief tutorial(s).

|   | TUTORIAL TITLE | URL |
|---|---|---|
| 1 |  |  |
| 2 |  |  |
| 3 |  |  |

## Activity 6-7: Learn Something New with an Online Tutorial

Select a brief tutorial you listed in Activity 6-6. Complete the tutorial and show you have learned about the topic or task by generating a product consistent with what you have learned. For example, if you took a tutorial on creating web pages using HTML, create a simple web page using HTML. If you need help thinking of a way to present what you've learned, ask your instructor.

# 7 Having Fun the Internet Way— Entertainment

## Focus

Are we having fun yet?                                              —Carol Burnett

## Overview

What forms does entertainment take on the Internet? You can get an idea by looking for entertainment links on a search tool web site (Figure 1). We have explored some means of having fun on the Internet, like community and shopping. In this lesson, we will examine a few others.

With the Internet, you don't need to buy a newspaper or make a lot of phone calls to plan your weekend. You can learn about movies, concerts, sporting events, and other local events and buy tickets online. You can download your favorite songs to play again and again and listen on your computer to broadcasts from radio stations around the world.

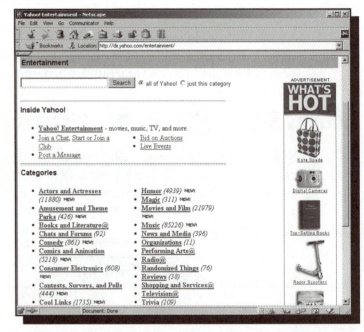

Figure 1 Yahoo!® Entertainment Categories

People once played computer games only on their own computers. Now they can connect through the Internet and play online with others, from web-based versions of television game shows to advanced 3-D interactive games. You can download free demos of games, as well as all kinds of games that are inexpensive or free.

In this lesson, you'll find out how to use the Net to plan your next trip, from leaving your driveway to arriving at Aunt Betty's 500 miles later. You will learn about **virtual tours**—visiting Australia's Great Barrier Reef, for instance, without even getting your feet wet. You will also learn where to find a good read online.

## Books, Magazines, and Newspapers

As you learned in Lesson 2, many magazines and newspapers have web sites. At these sites, you can follow the latest news from around the world. You can read full-length features from your favorite magazines. You can check out a good book at web sites like the Internet Public Library (http://www.ipl.org) and Bartleby.com (http://bartleby.com).

# Local Events

The Internet is a growing source of information about concerts, plays, movies, sporting events, and other happenings in and around town. For example, at Yahoo!® you can select the **Movies** link, key your ZIP Code or city and state, and get movie listings and show times for participating theaters. Categorical indexes, along with sites like http://www.moviefone.com and sites for local theaters or chains, provide movie reviews, driving directions, maps, and prices. At some sites, you can purchase tickets online and even print them on your printer.

At http://www.culturefinder.com (Figure 2), you can find out about and purchase tickets for plays, concerts, art exhibits, and other cultural events for many communities. Tired of driving or waiting on the phone to buy tickets for an event? You can purchase them online from Ticketmaster at http://www.ticketmaster.com. Many theaters, symphonies, and sports teams have web sites with similar services and more. Newspaper web sites are yet another resource for finding out what's going on around town.

Figure 2 CultureFinder.com

# Music

With the advent of the World Wide Web and its multimedia capabilities, audio delivery via the Internet has grown. There are two main mechanisms for delivering audio on the Internet: downloading static audio clips and receiving streaming audio.

Downloading static audio clips was the first delivery mechanism for music and other types of audio. It involves **digitizing** a music clip or other type of audio clip, or translating it into a format the computer can play. Static audio clips are files that people can download from a web site and play on their computer systems. The most common static formats are *.wav, .mid,* and *.mp3.*

Static sound clips may be **linked** to web pages (people click an object on the page to listen to them) or **embedded** in web pages (they play automatically). In either case, the files are downloaded to the user's hard drive and played by a media application on the computer, such as the Microsoft® Windows Media™ Player. Unfortunately, these audio files are often quite large and

require substantial time to download before playing. To remedy this download issue, streaming audio formats and applications have been developed.

**Streaming audio** takes a sound clip and sends it to your computer in a continuous data stream. The streaming application software does not have to wait until the entire audio clip is downloaded before it can play the sound. The data stream is **buffered** into your computer (a portion is saved to your computer). Once enough data has been delivered to start playing, the audio clip will play.

Depending on the speed of your Internet connection, your streaming audio clip may occasionally stop to "buffer in" more data before continuing to play. The size of the file is not as big an issue in this type of delivery, as the sound can play as the rest of the file is downloaded. Two of the most popular streaming formats are the RealAudio® format and the Microsoft® Windows Media™ Format. Figure 3 shows a RealPlayer® digital media software application for listening to RealAudio® format streaming media clips.

**Figure 3 RealPlayer® Digital Media Software Application**

If you do not have a player for streaming media, you can download one for free. For the Microsoft® Windows Media™ Player, visit the Microsoft® web site at http://www.microsoft.com. The RealPlayer® digital media software application can be obtained from RealNetworks at http://www.real.com.

Because of its high sound quality, the *.mp3* format has become very popular. To find *.mp3* files on the Internet, use the advanced search engine features you learned about in Lesson 1. AltaVista, for example, allows you to do an advanced search just for *.mp3* files. Advanced search features allow you to quickly locate audio clips that interest you. Many sites offer these sound files for free.

Streaming media is an exciting technology. It not only can stream static audio clips to your computer but can

**Figure 4 Rock Radio Stations**

also send live audio and/or video to your computer. Many radio stations offer live streaming audio of their programming. Figure 4 shows a list of some rock radio stations, with a searchable index to thousands more. You can also use search tools to locate online radio stations. If you are out of town, you can listen to your favorite radio station online from anywhere in the world. Are you learning Spanish? Connect to a Mexican radio station and test your translation ability. The possibilities are endless!

# Games

Games abound on the Internet. You can download and install games on your computer. You can play them online. You can play with others using the Internet as your connection medium. There are many possibilities.

You can get free demos for many games on the Internet. Download a demo, install it, and play it. Did you like it? You can order the full game online or buy it at a local store. You can also find online reviews by experts, consumer groups, and users to help you make a choice.

You will find a wealth of shareware and freeware games on the Internet. **Shareware** is software that you can use free for a trial period, often 30 days, after which you have to register the software, usually for a nominal fee. **Freeware** is free for use. Visit a shareware and freeware archive site, such as http://download.cnet.com (choose the **Games** link). Notice in Figure 5 the extensive index of shareware and freeware games.[1]

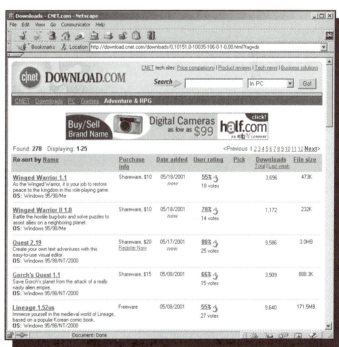

Figure 5  Games for Download at CNET.com

Don't want to download and install a game and want a variety to choose from? Many search engine web sites have direct links to games ranging from solitaire to crosswords and more.

Most popular television game shows have web-based versions that you can play online for free. For example, online versions of *Jeopardy!*® and *Wheel of Fortune*® are hosted on the Sony® entertainment web site The Station® (http://www.station.sony.com). Some game-show sites even provide monetary awards to top players. There are games for children's shows as well, such as the popular preschool show, *Blue's Clues*® (http://www.nickjr.com).

---

[1] Reprinted with permission from CNET, Inc. Copyright ©1995–2000 www.cnet.com. Screen shot taken May 30, 2001.

On the Internet, you can play many games, especially advanced and complex games, against people on other computers. Players may be across the street or around the world. You purchase such a game, install it on your computer, and go to a gaming server web site. A **gaming server** is a central computer that acts as an intermediary, allowing several computers to connect to the same gaming environment so users can play within the same game world or interface. You can use search engines to find gaming servers. If you have a technical background, you can even make a direct connection between your computer and a friend's computer across the Internet without the need for a gaming server.

For some online games, you may need an application such as the Macromedia® Flash™ Player and the Macromedia® Shockwave® Player. You can download these applications from the Internet for free. Downloading files will be addressed in Lesson 10.

## Travel

As you have learned, the Internet is a wonderful resource for travel. You can take a virtual trip online through picture galleries and videos. You can plan travel with Internet tools. You can pay for tickets and other travel expenses online, often with substantial savings.

**Virtual Travel.** You can travel "virtually" anywhere in the world, without leaving the comfort of your own home. For example, at http://www.buzzlondon.com, you can tour greater London (England) with photos and even navigate through the city by a map. Virtual tours can include video images from **WebCams,** or web-based cameras. They are located all over the world and show you real-time pictures. How about an aerial view of your hometown? Check out http://terraserver.microsoft.com.

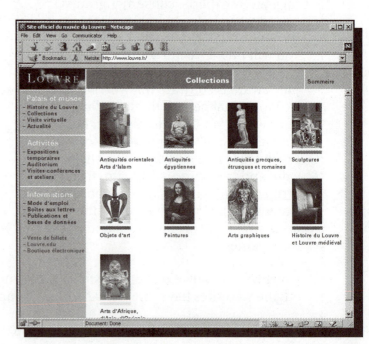

Figure 6 Page from the Louvre Web Site

Hundreds of museums have web sites. Most provide virtual tours. How often can you get to the Louvre in Paris, France (Figure 6), to see the *Mona Lisa* or other art and artifacts? You can visit the museum in a virtual environment, see the works up close in vivid photography, and even simulate walking through the museum.

**Trip Planning.** As you learned in Lesson 2, the Internet is *the* place to plan a vacation. You can find places to visit, descriptions and photos, detailed maps, advice on what to bring and wear, write-ups of attractions—in short, everything that a print travel guide could provide and more. Travel sites like http://www.frommers.com or http://www.expedia.com or categorical indexes are good starting points for this kind of research.

Suppose you are planning a road trip. At trip planner web sites like http://www.freetrip.com, you can enter a destination and get detailed directions, road maps, and even lists of motels, restaurants, and places of interest both for your destination and along the way. What once required an up-to-date atlas, printed travel guides, and telephoning now only requires the Internet and the address where you are going.

**Travel Purchases.** Buying plane or train tickets used to require the help of a travel agent or hours on the telephone. Today, tickets, cruise packages, car rentals, and many other travel purchases can be made online, through general travel web sites like http://www.travelocity.com (Figure 7) or web sites of individual vendors like Delta Air Lines or Amtrak®. A categorical index is a good starting point for finding these vendors.

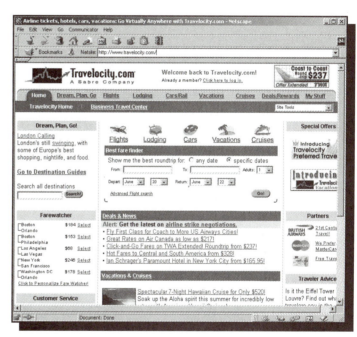

Figure 7 Travelocity.com

The Internet offers budget travel sites where you can search for low airfares, hotel rates, and so on. As you know, some travel sites allow you to set a price you want to pay for an airline ticket or other travel purchase and contact you by e-mail when the item is available at that price. You can also get travel bargains at an auction or price selection site, such as http://www.priceline.com. At these sites, you set the price you are willing to pay, and travel vendors offer you deals based on your price.

# Conclusion

There are many types of entertainment on the Internet. This lesson focused on just a few. You can use the Internet to get information on movies and other local events. You can download music and listen to far-flung radio stations. You can find all kinds of games and play online against others. You can plan perfect vacations and read great newspapers, books, and magazines. The Internet offers endless opportunities for having fun.

## Activity 7-1: Plan Entertainment Around Town

1. You are taking a friend out. Use Internet tools to get the following information:

   a. Find a movie that is playing locally that you would like to see. Print a review and view a multimedia clip, if available.

   b. How much are two tickets to a Friday evening show? _____

   c. Can you buy tickets online? _____

   d. Print or copy down directions for getting to the movie theater.

2. Create a simple spreadsheet or table in which you calculate the cost of the evening. Include the approximate price for dinner at a restaurant you like, $0.10 per mile for gas, and any other expenses, such as a snack at the movie.

## Activity 7-2: Get Audio and Video

1. Use a media application to listen to three streaming media clips. Write down the names of the clips. Put an asterisk (*) by the one you liked best.

   _____

   _____

   _____

2. Use Internet search tools to find a WebCam. Visit one or more virtual locations or events. Write a paragraph describing what you viewed. Include the site URL.

3. Use the Internet to identify four radio stations in other countries that you might like that offer live streaming audio of their programming.

| NAME OF STATION | COUNTRY |
|---|---|
|  |  |
|  |  |
|  |  |
|  |  |

# Activity 7-3: Find Online Games

1. Locate two sites where you can play games online. Record their URLs below.

   _____

   _____

2. Find a demo for a game that interests you. Record the URL and name of the game.

   URL: _____

   Name: _____

3. Find one shareware or freeware game that interests you. Record the URL, name of the game, and price, if appropriate.

   URL: _____

   Name: _____

   Price (if appropriate): _____

4. Find a review of a game that interests you. Print the review.

5. Can you play games based on the *Star Wars*® movies online? _____

# Activity 7-4: Plan a Road Trip

Choose a city that is a day's drive away. Imagine you have a relative who lives there. Use a trip planning tool to plan a road trip to visit your relative. Print (1) driving directions, (2) maps, (3) a description of an attraction you would like to visit on the way, (4) a list of budget restaurants along the way, and (5) information about an economy hotel (including price) at a sensible stopping point on the way. Assume you are leaving Thursday and driving back Saturday (you will need a room for those two nights—you will stay with your relative when you arrive).

# Activity 7-5: Find Bargain Fares for Travel

Choose a place you would like to go that you could get to by air or train. Use Internet tools to find three good fares for travel three weeks from today and staying a week. Print your information. Figure the best choice for you. Write a short paragraph explaining your decision.

# 8 Digital Photography

## Focus

I really believe there are things nobody would see if I didn't photograph them.

—Diane Arbus

## Overview

We love to take pictures. We buy film, load the camera, and snap our photos. Then we run down to the drugstore to have them developed. Days later, we get our prints. If we want to share some of those pictures, it's back to the drugstore to order extra copies and then to the post office to mail them to friends and family.

Digital cameras are changing all that. You don't load the camera or develop film. You don't even *use* film. When you snap a picture, it is digitized into the camera memory or onto a removable computer disk or card. The digital image can then be downloaded to your computer. From there you can print copies on paper or send the image electronically to as many people as you like with the click of a mouse.

Many web hosting organizations provide you with a location for digital images—a digital photo gallery that visitors can browse to keep up with what you are doing. If you use print film, you can pay a few dollars extra to have printed pictures digitized. You can edit your digital images and have them converted to printed pictures or even 35mm slides. This lesson will explore some of the ways that the Internet is being used to facilitate digital photography.

## Digital Cameras

As you might guess, some of the earliest users of digital cameras were professional photographers. It didn't take long for photojournalists to discover them. Scientists, particularly astronomers, have relied on digital images for years. The Hubble Space Telescope uses digital sensors to capture magnificent images from space. Figure 1 shows a photo taken by the Space Telescope of a galaxy estimated to be tens of millions of light-years away. In the Mars Rover mission, a small robot vehicle crawled along the surface of Mars, taking pictures with a digital camera and sending them to earth by radio transmission.

The rapid growth of web sites for businesses and other organizations has been accompanied by a rise in digital camera use among all sorts of workers. For example, increasing numbers of people are searching for homes on the web. Realtors take digital pictures of houses and post them on listings web sites. Teachers and company public relations personnel are other examples.

Figure 1 **Digital Photo of a Distant Galaxy**

What can *you* do with a digital photo? You can send it as an e-mail attachment, without any sort of developing, directly to family members and friends. You can insert it in a word-processed or desktop-published document. You can post it on your own personal home page or in an online gallery open to all or selected viewers (more about these later). You can photograph items you want to sell in online auctions. You can preserve and share aging family photographs by having a photo processing service create digital versions of them (more about this below).[1]

Digital cameras are dropping in price, so you can buy a better camera with more features for less money. Cameras range in cost from less than $100 to more than $1,000. The more expensive cameras capture images at a better resolution (measured in **pixels**) than the less expensive ones. The low end for acceptable picture quality is probably 640 × 480 pixels. This resolution is good enough for e-mailing pictures to friends and posting them on the web. For other uses, such as enlarged or detailed printed images, you may need a camera with higher resolution.

# Photo Processing Web Sites

Where there were once just a few online photo processing web sites, there are now numerous companies that provide a variety of printing services. These services range from film-to-digital formatting to digital-to-print formatting and more. Figure 2 shows the photo developing site, dotPhoto.

Film-to-digital formatting has become big business in the last several years. Previously, if you wanted to get a printed photograph into a digital format, you had to use a scanner. Today, many photo processing web sites will digitize your photos and send them to you on a CD-ROM or store them on an Internet-connected server. Instead of running down to the drugstore for your pictures, you can log in to this server with a password and download them directly to your computer. The quality and resolution of these digital images are usually quite good, and the cost is minimal. What once required the purchase of an expensive scanner now only requires a few dollars extra on your film processing order.

Figure 2 **Photo Processing Web Site**

---

[1] The source for some of the information in this discussion is Dennis Curtain, "How Digital Cameras Are Being Used," http://www.shortcourses.com/how/world/world.htm (21 April 2001).

Digital-to-print formatting is another popular service. You can upload your digital photos and order prints. Some photo processing sites have free plug-ins to streamline the uploading process. Prices for a 4 × 6 print are generally 50 cents or less.

Photo processing web sites offer other useful options. Some give you space to store and organize your photos online. Some provide simple image editing tools (more on these below). Some sites sell gift items that you can have personalized with your photos, such as hats, T-shirts, and calendars.

## Business Service Sites

Other services convert digital images to more traditional formats like flyers, posters, and slides. Business presentation services can take a presentation created with an application like the Microsoft® PowerPoint® presentation graphics program and convert it into high-quality 35mm slides. These services have been available for years, but the response time has dramatically improved with increased access to the Internet. You can submit your presentation file to a company such as Genigraphics (Figure 3) as an e-mail attachment and have the 35mm slides generated and delivered to your office by the next business day.

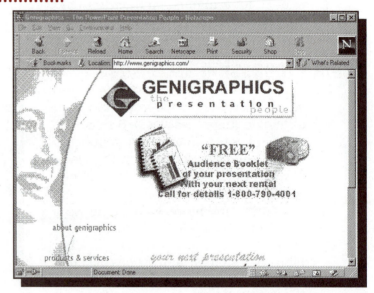

Figure 3 The Genigraphics Web Site

## Editing Images

Like other computer art files, digital photographs can be edited. Instead of taking a negative into a darkroom and immersing it in chemicals, you can take a digital photograph into a paint or photo editing program and get many of the same effects and more with the lights on. For example, you can crop the picture to show just the part you want. You can add text and adjust the color, brightness, or contrast. You can apply filters to make the picture look like an oil painting or watercolor. You can even "stitch" different pictures together and get rid of the annoying red-eye problem.

There are many different programs, including shareware and freeware, that you can use to edit digital photographs. You will find easy-to-use paint programs such as Jasc® Paint Shop Pro™, as well as sophisticated editing software such as Adobe® Photoshop®. Many digital cameras come with basic image editing software.

**Digital Photography**

# Clip Art Galleries

Besides taking your own digital photos, you can obtain digital photos in clip art collections on the web and on CD-ROMs. You should be aware of copyright and other restrictions on use associated with many photos. Carefully read and comply with any terms of use. Some web sites offer photos that are in the public domain. These photos can be used without restriction. You must get permission to use any photos protected by copyright, unless the site says otherwise. You must also obtain permission to scan copyrighted photos.

# Personal Photo Galleries

Imagine creating a gallery of your favorite photos online, which you can make available to everyone or to selected family members and friends. Web **portals** (sites that offer a variety of services, such as e-mail, chat rooms, search engines, and shopping) provide space for both online galleries and storage of other types of files free of charge.

For example, Yahoo!® provides registered users with a storage location called the Briefcase. When you create your Yahoo!® account, you automatically get e-mail services, a Briefcase storage location, and instant messaging capabilities. Your Briefcase is located at http://briefcase.yahoo.com/*accountname*.

The Briefcase is a general storage area, about 25MB in size that can contain many folders and photo albums that you create. You can provide open access to your folders and albums or limit access. Excite® uses a web presence called Webshots, at http://www.webshots.com, to provide photo gallery storage locations. Photo processing web sites offer similar services to customers.

The process for creating and sharing your own gallery is simple:

1. Gather your images in a digital format, by taking them with a digital camera, getting them from clip art galleries, scanning them, or paying a service to convert your print pictures.

2. Set up your gallery location through a provider such as Yahoo!® or Webshots (Excite®).

3. Use your provider's upload feature to upload the photos to the hosting server.

4. Set your access permissions (unrestricted or restricted) to the photo gallery.

5. Announce the web site location to family members and friends.

## Galleries of Art and Photography

Thousands of art and photo galleries exist on the Internet. You can find these galleries by using search tools. If you are interested in a particular style or school of art, such as Surrealism, you might begin by searching for art galleries or museums and then search within a gallery or museum site for that specific type of art. Or you may want to search for specific Surrealist artists, such as Salvador Dali. You may find web sites for brick-and-mortar museums that focus entirely on that artist, such as the Salvador Dali Museum web site at http://www.salvadordalimuseum.org. Another location would be an independently run web site devoted to the artist, such as http://www.dali-gallery.com (Figure 4).

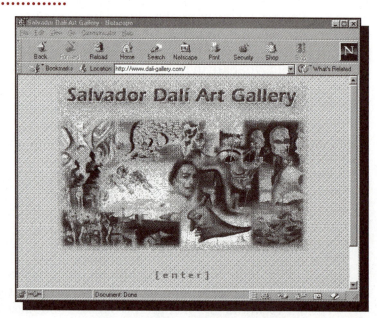

Figure 4 **Salvador Dali Site**

Another great way to locate galleries of art and photography is to use a categorical index. These sites usually include categories for art and photography. Browse the indexes and locate the specific type of art or photo gallery you are trying to find.

## Photography Contests and Communities

Photographers and artists are usually looking for ways to share their work. The Internet is providing a new avenue for them to show the world their talents. Individuals desiring to display their work can either create their own web site or enter a photo or art contest. These contests are like traditional competitions, but the work is in digital form and therefore is in many ways easier to display. The primary method for finding such contests is search tools. Photo processing web sites also sometimes offer photo contests to draw business.

In Lesson 5, you learned how people are using the Internet to build online communities with others who share their interests. Photography and art-related groups have begun to multiply. Members share information and tips on their craft and on how to get work shown. They offer suggestions and comments on each other's work and much more. The Internet provides a wonderful medium for individuals with similar interests to join together (virtually) and share thoughts and ideas.

**Digital Photography**

# Online Greeting Cards

A final way that you can use digital photography and art on the Internet is through online greeting cards. Many web sites provide a selection of greeting cards for birthdays, holidays, and so on, just like the cards that you buy in a store. You can select a card and customize it with your own personal message and sometimes music or a voice recording as well. The system will generate and store the card on its server and send an e-mail to the recipient, who can then view the card on the server at his or her leisure.

Figure 5 **The Blue Mountain Web Site**[2]

Many sites offer online greeting cards, from booksellers to museums to sites devoted exclusively to cards. Blue Mountain (http://www.bluemountain.com), shown in Figure 5, American Greetings (http://www.americangreetings.com), and Hallmark (http://www.hallmark.com) are some examples. Cards are usually free.

With greeting card software, you can create virtual greeting cards with your own artwork or photographs. These can then be printed and mailed to recipients or e-mailed and viewed directly on their computers. You can get greeting card software as shareware and freeware. You can also create virtual greeting cards in paint, desktop publishing, and even word processing software.

# Conclusion

The Internet offers powerful tools for people to create, edit, use, and share digital photographs. You can obtain film-to-digital images or digital images in a printed format. You can have digital files made into 35mm slides, printed flyers, or even posters and have them delivered to your office the next day. You can edit and e-mail photos and create online galleries to share your work with others. You can enter contests and join online communities of artists and photographers. All of this and more is provided through the powerful communication network we call the Internet (and the World Wide Web).

# Activity 8-1: Get Digital Photos

1. Use a digital camera to take at least half a dozen photos and upload them to your computer. If you do not have access to a digital camera, you may scan your own personal print photos or obtain photos from a clip art site. Make sure you do not scan copyrighted materials and that you read and follow any terms of use for photographic clip art. An excellent resource for downloadable public domain photos is the Multimedia Gallery at the National Aeronautics & Space Administration (NASA) web site (http://www.nasa.gov).

2. Print your photos and e-mail one as an attachment to your instructor and two classmates.

# Activity 8-2: Edit a Photo

Choose one of your photos from Activity 8-1 and edit it. You can use image editing software that came with your digital camera, a basic paint program, or any suitable software you have available or that you can download from the Internet. Crop the photo and try at least one other effect. Print your best results.

# Activity 8-3: Create an Online Photo/Art Gallery

Using the photos you obtained in Activity 8-1, create a photo gallery. Use the Webshots service of Excite® or another similar service. Upload your images and share the address with your instructor, family members, and friends.

# Activity 8-4: Locate Photo Services Providers

Pair up with another student. Using your searching skills, locate two photo processing web sites. Compare the features of the two sites. Look at items like these:

- How easy the site is to use
- The process for uploading photos
- Prints—price and method and speed of delivery
- Whether the site offers personalized gifts, online photo albums, and/or editing tools
- Any other features you think are important

Write a several-paragraph review of the two sites.

**Digital Photography**

# Activity 8-5: Price Business Services

Visit Genigraphics or a similar business service site. Determine the cost for a set of twelve 35mm slides, including delivery. Choose a delivery time (next business day, for example). Compose and key a memo to your instructor explaining the costs, the procedure for sending files, and when and how you would receive your slides or prints.

# Activity 8-6: Find Art and Photo Galleries

Using your search skills, locate URLs for three art and/or photo galleries that interest you. Record the names of the galleries and their URLs below. Print an image from one of these galleries. Write a paragraph about the image.

|   | GALLERY | URL |
|---|---------|-----|
| 1 |         |     |
| 2 |         |     |
| 3 |         |     |

# Activity 8-7: Find Communities

Locate and record the URLs for three art- and/or photography-related communities on the Internet. These can be discussion groups, sharing groups, special interest groups, etc.

|   | URL |
|---|-----|
| 1 |     |
| 2 |     |
| 3 |     |

# Activity 8-8: Send Virtual Cards

Send a virtual card to your instructor. Send one to yourself to see how the process works.

# 9 Investing and Money Management

## Focus

You have ten shares of each of the following stocks. Go to Yahoo!® (http://www.yahoo.com) and select the **Finance** link. Find the name of the company and the current price per share. How much is your stock worth today?

| TICKER SYMBOL | COMPANY | PRICE PER SHARE | VALUE OF TEN SHARES |
|---|---|---|---|
| PSUN | | | |
| HSY | | | |
| SCHL | | | |

## Overview

As of January 2000, some 7 million American households were investing online. The Internet has completely changed investing, both who is investing and how they are doing it. Brokers have traditionally charged high fees for the personal services they provide. You can set up investment accounts with online brokers and handle your own investments for reasonable fees. The Internet provides a wealth of resources for conducting investment research and maintaining a portfolio. It also offers a wide variety of valuable tools that you can use to enhance your investment opportunities.

While the ability to trade online is new, the fundamentals of sound investment and money management have not changed. The Internet gives you the ability to assemble the information you need to make sound investment decisions easily and quickly.

## Investment Research

Investment research comes in all shapes and sizes. You may need to keep up with any news about the companies that you are investing in. You may also need to review the financial documents of an organization before you decide to invest in it. You may need a basic explanation of investing or expert advice on what to buy. Regardless of the type of research you need to conduct, the Internet is likely to have the resources you need.

**Company Web Sites.** For research on a particular company, the place to start is the company's web site. Most companies provide up-to-date financial reports and other useful information online for current or potential investors. You can use search tools to find a company web site.

You can also try keying the company name in the URL as you learned in Lesson 1: http://www.companyname.com.

**Categorical Indexes.** Many categorical indexes such as Yahoo!® have direct links to their own financial web pages. These pages offer a wide variety of useful features for investors, such as the following:

- Stock quotes

- Ticker symbol (trading code) lookup

- Latest financial news, including news linked to specific stocks

- Graphs showing performance trends for stocks over five or more years

- Screening tools that recommend stocks based on specific criteria

- Information and quotes on mutual funds, bonds, and dozens of other types of investments

- Educational information about financial terms, concepts, and how to analyze financial investments

**Financial "Supersites."** There are also financial "supersites" that offer a wide variety of useful information for investors, such as The Motley Fool® (http://www.fool.com), shown in Figure 1; the MoneyCentral™ personal finance online service (http://moneycentral.msn.com), a Microsoft®-hosted site; and SmartMoney.com (http://www. smartmoney.com).

**Business Sites.** Other web sites focus on providing all types of information about and for businesses, including financial information. These sites usually offer some basic information about a company, with more detailed information available for a fee. Hoovers Online® at http://www.hoovers.com is an excellent example of such a site. A similar site is Multex Investor at http://www.multexinvestor.com.

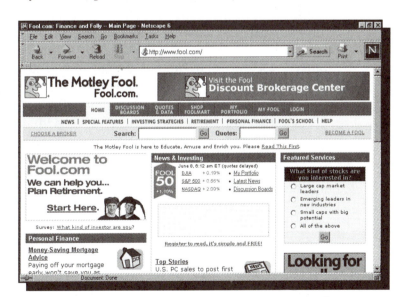

Figure 1 **The Motley Fool® Web Site**

**E-mail Newsletters.** E-mail newsletters are another good source of investment information. You learned about e-mail newsletters in Lesson 5. Many good investment newsletters are available on the Internet. You can subscribe to them and have them delivered directly to your e-mail account. Some of these newsletters are free, while others charge a fee. A good example of a free newsletter would be *The Day Ahead,* available at http://www.zdnet.com/zdii/lists/theday ahead/subscribe.html.

**Investment Comparison Tools.** Many financial web sites, such as the MoneyCentral™ site, offer a useful tool that allows you to compare investments side by side. You can select a number of stocks, mutual funds, or other investments that you are interested in and instruct the web site to show you a comparison of them. The resulting web page displays a side-by-side comparison of major features of the selected investments.

# Portfolio Tracker Tools

Many web portals and financial sites such as Kiplinger.com (http://www.kiplinger.com) and Money.com (http://www.money.com) provide a portfolio tracker tool that lets you create and manage online investment portfolios. For example, if you belong to Yahoo!® you can create one or more investment portfolios and display them on your My Yahoo!® customized web page.

When you create a portfolio in Yahoo!® you enter the ticker symbols for your holdings and check off any other details you want included, such as the number of shares you bought and the price you paid. The portfolio tracker tool retains this information. Each time you access your portfolio, the tracker tool automatically updates it with the latest price per share, and total value of your portfolio, as well as any other details you chose. You can see the position, value, and performance of your investment portfolio at a glance. Clicking the portfolio name yields the usual Yahoo!® display of investment information, but it is customized for the stocks in your portfolio.

Since these portfolios are not directly linked to a brokerage account, you can create portfolios of investments that you do not actually own. This allows you to test investments for a period of time before committing to them. Some online portfolio systems can even track stocks for you and alert you by e-mail when a stock hits a high or low price that you set.

A similar feature provided by some online brokerage firms is a customizable web page for keeping track of your investments. These pages are usually housed on a brokerage company's web server. They allow you not only to track the stocks you have in your portfolio but also to insert other key web page sections such as specific market-related news, research links, and current quotes.

# Investing Online

Once you decide you are ready to begin making online investments, you will need to find a good online broker. A **broker** is a person or company that acts as an intermediary to buy and sell investments (e.g., stocks and bonds) on your behalf for a fee. Many of the traditional brick-and-mortar brokers also provide online trading options. Although they often charge slightly more per trade, these brokers provide personal services and research information to assist you in making good, informed investment decisions.

Discount brokers typically are less expensive and offer fewer services and less assistance. If price is a factor, if you are an experienced investor, or if you are confident about making trading decisions on your own, you may wish to use a discount broker.

Research the online trading companies. Look at more than just the per-trade cost for the online account. Hidden fees can cost you greatly down the road. Make sure you find out how much support and investment advice you get with your trading account. Ameritrade® (http://www.ameritrade.com), shown in Figure 2, Datek (http://www.datek.com), Charles Schwab (http://www.schwab.com), and E*TRADE (http:// www.etrade.com) are some examples of online investment brokers.

Online brokerage firms provide you with many services. Here are just a few:

- Real-time stock quotes

- Stock purchases

- Margin buying (paying for stocks, bonds, or other investments by borrowing money from a broker)

- Market orders (orders to buy or sell immediately at the best price available)

- Investing tools

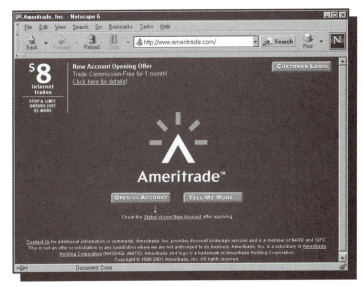

Figure 2 **The Ameritrade® Web Site**

Suppose you are unfamiliar with stock trading. Many online brokers have trading demos to walk you through the process. Some examples of sites that offer this feature are Ameritrade®, CSFB*direct* (http://www.csfbdirect.com), and Charles Schwab.

Many respected financial sites offer ratings of online brokers. These include Barron's Online (http://www.barrons.com), Kiplinger.com, and Money.com.

# Money Management

No financial discussion would be complete without exploring the wealth of money management information and tools available online. You can use financial planning sites to set your personal financial goals and to make practical plans to meet them. A good place to begin is at a personal finance hub like Money.com, the MoneyCentral™ personal finance online service; SmartMoney.com; or Quicken.com (http://www.quicken.com). These sites offer a wide range of resources on insurance, home financing, taxes, retirement, banking, budgeting, credit, and other topics.

**Banks.** Many banks and other financial institutions are now online, providing customers with the ability to fully manage their accounts, pay bills, research loan rates, and apply for loans and credit cards, all online. Personal help is also available and only an e-mail away.

**Cars and Homes.** You have already learned how helpful the Internet can be when you are in the market for a car. If you are buying a house, you will find that in many areas real estate listings are online, complete with detailed descriptions, clickable street maps, exterior and interior photos, and even videos. Many sites provide online calculators that you can use to figure your estimated monthly cost for a mortgage.

**Insurance.** Looking for insurance? The information is just a mouse-click away with the Internet. You can find information on life, car, home, and other insurance online. Sites like InsWeb® (http://www.insweb.com), insure.com (http://www.insure.com), Kiplinger.com, and SmartMoney.com provide you with expert advice on the kind and amount of insurance you need. You can get tips on choosing a good insurance company and helpful tools. You can also get and compare quotes online.

Although some sites will provide you with an estimated quote online, most will require you to complete an online form that will be sent to an agent who will in turn e-mail you a quote. This is necessary because of how individual circumstances affect insurance costs—for business insurance, for example, the location of a property, the amount of the property a business uses, the building construction, etc.

**Credit Cards.** The Internet has many resources for credit card users. You can get general advice and explanations of features and terms such as APR. The Internet offers tips on using credit wisely and even credit card debt reduction strategies. You can also apply for credit cards online and find out if you are approved in a very short time. If you want to check your credit history before you apply, you can do that too. For less than $10, you can get your credit report online in seconds.

If you already have a credit card, or will have one shortly, you will be happy to know that you can also use the Internet to manage your credit card account. Many financial institutions allow you to access your credit card account through the web and obtain information such as current balance, credit line, and purchase history. You can also pay your credit card bill online with an electronic funds transfer. These features give you flexibility in managing your credit card account.

**Savings.** Perhaps you need to set savings goals for milestones such as college and retirement, as well as to do some estate planning. In addition to the financial planning supersites, organizations such as The Vanguard Group (http://www.vanguard.com), T. Rowe Price (http://www.troweprice.com), John Hancock (http://www.hancock.com), and Fidelity.com (http://www.fidelity.com) offer a helpful array of financial planning tools, such as interactive worksheets, special calculators for retirement needs and college costs, and tutorials.

**Taxes.** In 2000, more than 30 million individuals and tax preparers filed federal tax returns over the Internet. The Internal Revenue Service (IRS) web site at http://www.irs.gov makes tax preparation and online filing easy—or as easy as figuring your taxes ever can be! You can download tax forms and publications for the current and past tax years, click a flowchart to help determine your eligibility for deductions, and even pay online by authorizing direct transfer from a savings or checking account. For all kinds of information about taxes, it's hard to beat the award-winning web site TaxPlanet.com (http://www.taxplanet.com).

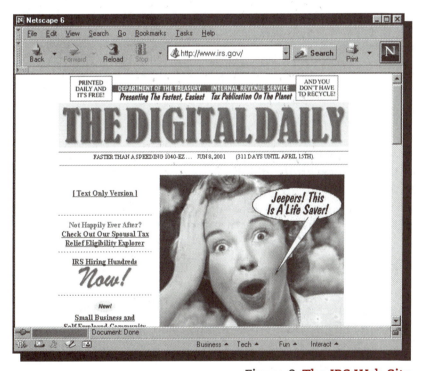

Figure 3 The IRS Web Site

# Conclusion

The Internet provides a wealth of invaluable tools for investment and personal money management. The Internet makes it easier to research investment opportunities, conduct financial transactions, and track investments. You can use Internet tools to manage your money better, from saving for college or retirement to banking and paying taxes. The Internet gives you, at little or often no cost, the tools you need for investing and personal finance decisions.

## Activity 9-1: Price Stocks

Use The Motley Fool®, the Microsoft® MoneyCentral™ personal finance online service, or Yahoo!® Finance to look up six companies whose products you use daily. Record their ticker symbols in the table along with the other information requested.

| COMPANY | TICKER SYMBOL | PRICE PER SHARE | COST FOR 50 SHARES |
|---|---|---|---|
|  |  |  |  |
|  |  |  |  |
|  |  |  |  |
|  |  |  |  |
|  |  |  |  |
|  |  |  |  |

## Activity 9-2: Research Stock Histories

Select two of the stocks that you looked up in Activity 9-1 and view the price history of each stock for the last year. Print a graph of the price history and write one or two paragraphs analyzing it. Were there any major changes? If so, investigate the history and news articles related to the stock. See if you can determine what happened to cause the stock price to change dramatically. Include this information in your paragraphs.

## Activity 9-3: Research Companies

Visit Hoover's Online® and view the Profile of the Day. Write a summary of the types of information that the profile provides. Additionally, write a short summary about the company being profiled. Include whether you would consider investing in the company and why or why not.

## Activity 9-4: Compare Investments

Select three stocks to compare from your list in Activity 9-1. Visit the MoneyCentral™ site and navigate to the **Investor** link. Under Stock Research, start the **Research Wizard.** Enter the ticker symbol for one of your stocks, click **Go,** and choose **Comparison.** Follow the directions to create a comparison of your three stocks. Although the directions suggest that you compare stocks in the same industry, you can compare any three stocks, whether they are in the same industry or not. Examine and print the resulting information. Write several paragraphs comparing and contrasting the three stocks. Which do you think would be the best investment?

# Activity 9-5: Understand Financial Terms

Many financial web sites have online glossaries of financial terms. These include The Motley Fool® and Yahoo!® Finance. Use one or more online financial glossaries to define the following terms:

1. bear market
2. bond
3. IPO (initial public offering)
4. limit order

5. mutual fund
6. P/E (price-to-earnings) ratio
7. security
8. shareholder

# Activity 9-6: Create a Portfolio

Go to a web portal or one of the financial sites mentioned in this lesson and use the portfolio tracking tool to create your own portfolio. Be sure to read the privacy statement and terms of use before submitting personal information to a site. If you are already a member of Yahoo!® you may wish to use its tool.

Add the stock ticker symbols for the six companies you identified in Activity 9-1. Have the site display the number of shares owned (pretend you have 100 shares of each stock). Watch the portfolio for the next week. How did it perform? Send an e-mail to your instructor that answers this question. Continue to watch your portfolio to see what it does.

# Activity 9-7: Explore Money Management Tools

1. Visit one of the personal finance hubs mentioned in this lesson. Try one of the interactive money management tools that interests you; e.g., a budget worksheet, college or retirement planner, or debt reduction tool. Print your results.

2. Use the Internet to research credit unions and banks. What are the differences? Which do you think you would prefer to use, and why? Write a paragraph that answers these questions.

3. Find an online bank or credit union that you would be eligible to join. If your current bank or credit union is online, you can use that organization. Make a list of the online services the bank or credit union offers.

# 10 Downloading Software

## Focus

Technology makes it possible for people to gain control over everything, except over technology.

—John Tudor

## Overview

In the past nine lessons, you have learned to use many different tools to obtain the information and resources from the Internet that you want and need. This lesson focuses on software. You can download all kinds of software from the Internet, on everything from small business management to golf. You can download updates for programs you already own, as well as utilities that will help you get more out of the Internet and keep your computer running smoothly.

The diversity of file types that you can download should cause you to keep a close eye on your computer and its susceptibility to viruses. A **virus** is a program or piece of code circulated maliciously through computer files that can damage or destroy files and software. At one time, computer viruses were only transmitted through executable files. Today, almost any type of computer file is susceptible to viral infection. This lesson discusses antivirus software (Figure 1) and other resources that you can get through the Internet.

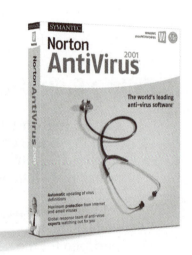

Figure 1
Norton AntiVirus® 2001

## Downloading Files from the Internet

The ability to download computer files has been inherent in the Internet since its inception. **File transfer protocol,** or FTP, was one of the first applications used on the Internet, and its purpose was to transfer files from one computer system across the Internet to another. The FTP process requires a server running FTP server software.

FTP is still very much used today. However, the FTP transfer process has largely been integrated into computer browsers. You click a hyperlink that reads "download file" or something similar, and the browser and web server initiate an FTP session to download the file to your computer.

The other primary way that users can download files is via HTTP—**Hypertext Transfer Protocol.** To set up computer files for HTTP download, the web designer uploads the files to a web server and creates links to them. When you click a link, the requested file is transported through your browser to your computer system using HTTP.

So what are you actually downloading? Games, music, media players, and images. Application software, updates, utilities, and much more. Whatever you are downloading, the process is the same: just find the link, complete any required information, and start the download. Let's talk about some popular types of downloads.

**Helper Applications.** Beginning Internet users, particularly, will occasionally need to download and install extra applications to access different types of information on the World Wide Web or other portions of the Internet. These **helper applications** include plug-ins and stand-alone software. They are usually the most-downloaded and most-needed "add-on" components for browsing the Internet.

**Plug-ins** are extra mini-applications or application code that interacts with your browser to provide it with added functionality. Plug-ins, for example, might enable your computer to play different types of audio or display different types of video. The Macromedia® Flash™ Player and the Macromedia® Shockwave® Player (http://www.macro media.com) are two very common plug-ins. These add-ins allow mini-applications created with Macromedia® multimedia development packages to run on your computer, providing you with a rich multimedia experience that would normally not be possible with a standard web page. Many online games require such plug-ins. Education tutorials are also created with these tools to give you a more media-rich educational experience (Figure 2).

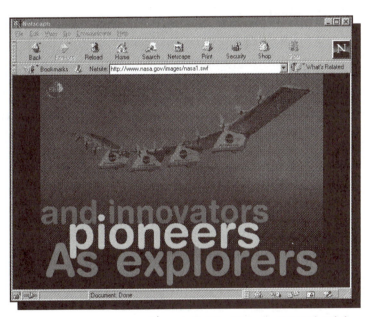

Figure 2 **The Movie NASA's Vision was created in Flash.**

How does a plug-in work? Suppose you choose to play a game that was formatted using Shockwave® software. First, you click the link to the file. Your browser automatically accesses the Shockwave® file on the page and runs the plug-in software to execute the file. The browser and plug-in work in cooperation to start the game and allow you to play it. To get the plug-in, you can often click a link on the web page or go to the manufacturer's web site.

Another extremely popular plug-in is the Adobe® Acrobat® Reader™, shown in Figure 3.[1] This plug-in allows your browser to display Portable Document Format (PDF) files. This file format is very popular because it works on many computer platforms and allows the viewer to see a document in its original format, including all graphics, layout features, text attributes, and more. Reports are often created as PDF files and linked to web pages for individuals to view. The PDF files can even be forms that you can fill in using your Adobe Acrobat Reader plug-in. Forms such as Internal Revenue Service (IRS) tax forms and job applications are often distributed in PDF format.

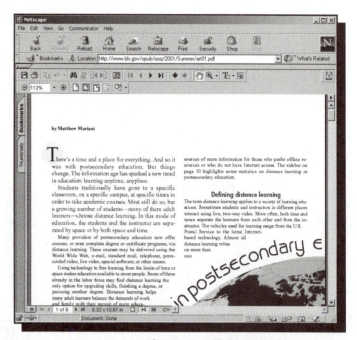

Figure 3 **Adobe Acrobat Reader**

Other helper applications are usually stand-alone software applications that can work with your browser or independently. Two good examples are the RealPlayer® digital media software application and Microsoft® Windows Media™ Player. These applications are multimedia players that can run independently if you want to view a video clip on your computer or listen to audio clips saved on your hard drive. However, they can also interface with your browser so that when you click the appropriate sound or video clip on a web page, the helper application (e.g., Microsoft® Windows Media™ Player) is started and the clip is downloaded by the browser and passed to the application to play.

**Full-featured Software.** In addition to helper applications, you can download full-featured application software from the Internet, including software you purchase, shareware, and freeware. If you are doing a lot of web page writing, for example, you may need a full-featured FTP software application. Visit a shareware/freeware archive and see what is available. Tucows™ (http://www.tucows.com) is one example of a shareware/freeware archive. CNET Shareware.com (http://shareware.cnet.com/) and CNET Download.com (http://download.cnet.com/) are similar sites.

If you need a specific application, you should visit the vendor's web site. For example, if you want to download and install a current version of the Netscape® browser suite, you would visit http://www.netscape.com and look for the link to download browsers.

**File Management.** When you start a download, a dialog box may appear asking whether you want to save the downloaded file to disk or open it (Figure 4). If you are downloading an appli-

---

[1] Abobe Acrobat Reader is ©1987–1999 Adobe Systems Incorporated. All rights reserved.

cation, you will probably want to save the file to its own folder on the hard drive, where you can run it later to install the software. The Save As dialog box will appear, prompting you for a location to save the file. *Make sure you save the file to a location where you can find it, and remember the filename!*

Consider creating a folder on your hard (C) drive called *downloads*. Every time you download a file, save it to this location. When you are ready to open the file you downloaded, browse to that folder and do so. Once an application has been installed, it is usually safe to delete the original file you downloaded. Using this process, you will always save to the same location, install, and delete the installation file so you do not clutter your download folder.

Before you install *any* software you download from the Internet, you should scan it for viruses with up-to-date antivirus software.

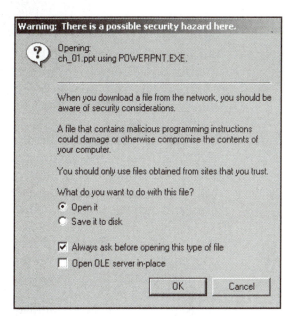

**Figure 4** Netscape® Download Dialog Box

# Virus Protection

Viruses are becoming more of a problem on the Internet every day. Just today (during the writing of this book) two virus alerts were sent out warning users of two new e-mail-based viruses. In the connected world of computers today, with the many ways that viruses can now replicate and be distributed, antivirus software for your computer is a must. It only takes one malicious virus to destroy the files on your computer.

A good antivirus program runs constantly when the computer is on. It scans inputs, outputs, downloads, program executions, and other system-related activities. It checks incoming e-mail and all files as they are opened, including downloads and attachments. It should give you the capability of running a full or partial scan manually anytime. It also permits you to install any service packs (bug fixes) or updates that become available (more on these below).

Your antivirus software should also have an auto-update feature for regularly updating the **virus string files,** or the listing of viruses your software can detect, to catch the latest viruses as they appear on the Internet. Most, but not all, major antivirus software vendors allow you to keep the virus string files updated for free. Some provide the service free for a year. Assuming you have this feature, you should regularly download updated files and install them to update your software—no later than monthly, and weekly is ideal. In some software, the auto-update feature does all the work for you—checking for updates and installing them automatically. You will learn more about this in the next part of the lesson.

Make sure the software you purchase can scan incoming e-mail messages. The majority of viruses today are being spread through e-mail message attachments, so it is critical that your antivirus software can also scan attachments as you open them, before they ever have a chance to infect your computer. You will greatly reduce your chances of getting a virus if you do not open e-mails from people you don't know or attachments that you did not expect to receive or that have unfamiliar names.

So where do you find this important software? You can visit your local computer or electronics store, or you can download it directly from the Internet. Make sure that the software is from a reliable antivirus software vendor such as Symantec® (Norton AntiVirus®— http://www.symantec.com) or McAfee® (VirusScan®—http://www. mcafee.com). Virus protection software ranges in price from $20 to $40.

If you don't have the software but think you might have a virus, is there anything you can do right away? Yes, some antivirus software vendors allow you to connect to their web site and run their virus checking software directly from the web site to check your hard drive. McAfee® offers a free trial of this service. Figure 5 displays the web page running the web-based virus scan. Notice the simplicity of the site and interface. You may also be able to download a free trial version of the software that you can use for a specified period of time, often 30, 60, or 90 days. Besides solving immediate virus problems, you can use free trials to compare antivirus software and decide which program to buy.

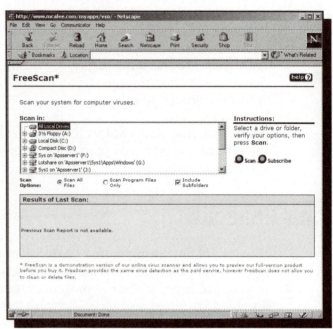

Figure 5 The McAfee® FreeScan Option

# Product Updates

With new software being released daily, it has become imperative to check for and install service packs or software updates. **Service packs** are software updates that are created after the original software was released for the purpose of fixing bugs in it. Individual software applications and even complete operating systems may require service packs to ensure proper operation.

At one time, service packs were issued on CD-ROMs and sent to the requesting individual. They might be offered free or for a minimal fee. Today, most service packs are distributed via the Internet. To get an update, you have to visit the company's web site, download the appropriate file(s), and install them on your hard drive. Many companies will also allow you to request a CD-ROM for a fee.

An increasing number of companies are putting auto-update features in their software to make it easier to update. These features require Internet access. The software application can be programmed to automatically check for and install updates on a regular basis. One example is Norton AntiVirus® with its *LiveUpdate*® feature (Figure 6). This feature can be set to check for updates daily, weekly, or monthly from the company's web site and to download and install any updates.

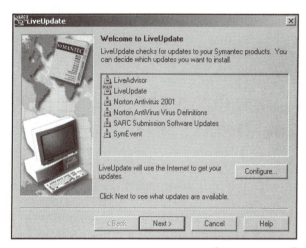

**Figure 6** Norton AntiVirus® *LiveUpdate*®

Some browsers also have auto-update features. The Netscape® *SmartUpdate*™ feature allows you to update only the browser files that need to be updated from the Netscape web site, so that you do not have to replace the entire software application. The feature analyzes your computer system and displays the browser version, software features, components, and plug-ins currently installed. It then provides a list of new browser features, components, and plug-ins that you can add.

Even operating systems are including these features. The Microsoft® Windows® 98 operating system and the latest Windows® products all have the *Windows® Update* option. When you select this option, *Windows® Update* connects to Microsoft's web site, analyzes your system, and determines whether any update files are needed. If so, it downloads the appropriate files and installs them on your hard drive.

Auto-update features are a great convenience compared to traditional methods for updating software. Without auto-update, you would need to determine if you need an update, find it manually, download the file, and run the setup executable file to install it. Automatic updates make updating your software much easier and more convenient. This is especially valuable for antivirus software.

For some software that you purchase, you can download additional or enhanced features. A good example is the online clip art gallery Design Gallery Live, hosted by Microsoft® for purchasers of some of its products. If you do not find the image you want in the software clip art gallery, you can click the **Clips Online** option and select from thousands of additional images online. These images can be added to your existing system clip art galleries.

Other software companies provide free software with the purchase of one of their software applications. Quicken® TurboTax® Deluxe, for example, has offered a free state version of their tax software that you could download from their web site. If you wanted a disk copy mailed to you, however, you were required to pay a fee.

Besides getting updates and additions for your software, you may need to find updated drivers for your hardware. The Internet has proven to be an excellent way for companies to deliver updated hardware drivers at virtually no cost.

# Online Computer Support and Resources

Obtaining support, updated hardware drivers, and other files from computer vendors used to be a tedious process. Today, it only requires you to visit the computer vendor's web site.

Most computer vendors maintain a support database on their web site that includes help questions that were previously asked and their solutions. These **knowledgebases** are invaluable to anyone trying to research a computer problem. Since you are likely not the only person to have experienced the problem you are having, your question has probably already been asked, answered, and stored in the knowledgebase.

If you did not find the answer to your problem in the knowledgebase, is there anywhere else you can go to get help without calling a technician on the telephone? Yes, many companies now offer live Internet-based help systems or e-mail links to technicians. The live systems use chat-style software to allow you to discuss your problem with a technician at the other end. Some even include a feature that lets the remote technician (with your permission) take control of your computer and show you something or check your settings to help troubleshoot the problem.

**Figure 7** HP™ Color LaserJet® 4500 Drivers and Downloads[2]

You may find that the solution to your problem is a system update or a new hardware driver. At the company web site, look for a link labeled **Drivers, Support,** or something similar. Then find the drivers you need, download them, and install them. Figure 7 shows the driver download page for Hewlett-Packard's HP™ Color LaserJet® 4500 series printers.

---

# Activity 10-5: Get Computer Support

Record the following information about your computer system and printer:

Computer brand: _____   Printer brand: _____

Computer model: _____   Printer model: _____

Locate the vendor web sites for your computer and printer. Find all current drivers for the computer and printer. Install the drivers, with your instructor's permission.

# Activity 10-6: Download Clip Art

If you have an application that provides an online clip gallery, such as Microsoft® Office Design Gallery Live, visit the online gallery and download at least five clip art images. If you do not have such an application, browse the Internet for free clip art and download at least five images.

# Activity 10-7: Use Adobe® Acrobat® Reader™

1. Visit the *Occupational Outlook Quarterly Online* (http://www.bls.gov/opub/ooq/ooqhome. htm). Browse the current issue or past issues in the Archives. Locate an article that interests you. You may wish to use the **Nutshell** and **Snippet** features to help you choose an article.

2. If you do not have Adobe Acrobat Reader, visit the Adobe web site at http://www.adobe.com, and download the free Adobe Acrobat Reader software. Make sure you get your instructor's permission first.

3. View the article online and print it.

4. Visit the IRS web site at http://www.irs.gov. Choose the **Forms & Pubs** and **Fill-in Forms** links. Select the *W-4 Employee's Withholding Allowance Certificate* form. Read the directions at the top of the form. Fill in the form on the computer and print it.

# Activity 10-8: Access Online Support

Locate the help/support web site for your word processing software. Identify the different types of support information available such as informational articles, online manuals, and tips. Find at least one helpful tip or suggestion for using your software and print it. Then try the tip or suggestion. Did it work?

# Quick Reference Guide

**Browsers**
http://www.microsoft.com/windows/ie
http://home.netscape.com/browsers
http://www.opera.com

**Search Engines**
http://www.altavista.com
http://www.google.com
http://www.excite.com
http://www.yahoo.com
http://www.search.com
http://www.go.com
http://www.looksmart.com
http://www.lycos.com
http://www.nbci.com
http://www.goto.com

**Meta Search Engines**
http://www.dogpile.com
http://www.askjeeves.com
http://debriefing.ixquick.com
http://www.metacrawler.com
http://www.mamma.com

**Internet Filtering Tools**
http://www.cybersitter.com/
http://www.surfcontrol.com/
http://www.netnanny.com/
http://securitysoft.com/

**Online Safety and Security**
http://www.getnetwise.org/
http://www.cyberangels.org/
http://www.safekids.com/
http://www.yahooligans.com/docs/safety

**Weather**
http://www.weather.com
http://www.intellicast.com/
http://www.weatherunderground.com/
http://www.rainorshine.com/

**People Searches**
http://www.classmates.com
http://people.yahoo.com
http://www.bigfoot.com/
http://www.411locate.com/
http://www.whowhere.lycos.com/

**Web-based Electronic Mail**
http://www.hotmail.com
http://www.yahoo.com
http://www.excite.com
http://www.lycos.com
http://www.eudora.com

**Instant Messaging**
http://www.icq.com
http://www.aol.com/aim/
http://www.yahoo.com/

**IRC Chat**
http://www.talkcity.com
http://chat.yahoo.com
http://www.mirc.com/

**Video/Audio Conferencing and Internet Phone**
http://www.microsoft.com/windows/netmeeting/
http://www.dialpad.com
http://www.net2phone.com/

**Reference and Research**
http://www.m-w.com
http://www.dictionary.com
http://dictionary.msn.com
http://www.yahoo.com (**Reference, Dictionaries**)
http://www.refdesk.com
http://www.britannica.com
http://encarta.msn.com
http://www.infoplease.com
http://www.discovery.com
http://www.studyweb.com
http://www.educationindex.com/
http://www.researchpaper.com

## Shopping

http://shopping.yahoo.com
http://www.mysimon.com
http://www.productreviewnet.com/
http://www.ebay.com

## Entertainment/Media

http://www.culturefinder.com
http://www.moviefone.com
http://www.amctheatres.com/
http://www.generalcinema.com/
http://www.uatc.com/
http://www.regalcinemas.com/
http://www.nowintheaters.com/
http://www.hollywood.com/
http://broadcast.yahoo.com
http://tv.yahoo.com

## Radio Stations

http://windowsmedia.com/radiotuner
http://www.streamaudio.com

## Travel & Trip Planning

http://www.travelocity.com
http://www.orbitz.com
http://www.expedia.com
http://www.frommers.com
http://www.concierge.com/
http://www.travelsearch.com/
http://www.bestfares.com/
http://www.discount-airfare.com/
http://www.mapquest.com
http://www.mapblast.com
http://www.freetrip.com
http://www.earthamaps.com/

## Financial Sites

http://www.yahoo.com (**Finance**)
http://www.fool.com
http://moneycentral.msn.com
http://www.smartmoney.com
http://www.kiplingers.com
http://www.money.com
http://www.quicken.com

## Online Brokers

http://www.ameritrade.com
http://www.etrade.com
http://www.datek.com
http://www.schwab.com
http://www.online.msdw.com
http://www.mldirect.ml.com/
http://www.quickandreilly.com/
http://www.buynhold.com
http://www.csfbdirect.com

## Plug-ins and Media Players

http://www.macromedia.com
http://www.adobe.com
http://www.real.com
http://www.microsoft.com

## Downloads and Updates

http://download.cnet.com/
http://shareware.cnet.com/
http://www.simtel.net/
http://www.tucows.com
http://www.microsoft.com
http://www.apple.com
http://www.sun.com
http://www.zdnet.com/

## AntiVirus

http://www.mcafee.com
http://www.symantec.com
http://www.f-secure.com/

## WebCam

http://www.earthcam.com/

# Index